VIGNY

Chatterton

Robin Buss

Lecturer in French,
Woolwich College of Further Education

Grant & Cutler Ltd
1984

© Grant & Cutler Ltd
1984
ISBN 0 7293 0170 2

I.S.B.N. 84-499-6900-X

DEPÓSITO LEGAL: V. 138 - 1984

Printed in Spain by
Artes Gráficas Soler, S.A., Valencia
for
GRANT & CUTLER LTD
11 BUCKINGHAM STREET, LONDON W.C.2

Contents

Preface   7

1. 'Cet ouvrage austère'   9

2. 'Fier, irritable et pauvre'   13

3. 'Martyrs et bourreaux'   22

4. 'L'action matérielle'   47

5. 'Un drame de la pensée'   55

6. 'Cette porte est ouverte à présent'   69

Bibliography and Sources   77

Preface

A guide book can be designed for reading either before, after or during the first visit to whatever it describes. This one assumes, from the third chapter onwards, that the reader will have some acquaintance with the plot and characters of Vigny's play, while the first two chapters give a brief account of its background and sources which does not necessarily assume any prior knowledge. In Chapter 3, I deal with the characters; in Chapter 4, with the development of the plot and with the structures of the drama; in Chapter 5, with themes, particularly that of the poet and his role in society. These three chapters make up the essential part of the guide, which ends with an assessment of the play in the context of later literature.

Throughout the guide, and particularly in the three central chapters, there are frequent page references to the Garnier-Flammarion edition of *Chatterton*, full details of which are given in the bibliography. Other works cited in the bibliography are indicated in the guide by a number, in italics, corresponding to the number attributed to them in the bibliography, followed by a page reference; for the Garnier-Flammarion *Chatterton* (numbered *1* in the bibliography), a page reference only is given. This edition of the play is readily available and I have chosen it in preference to others, such as the editions in the series of school texts published by Larousse, Didier or Bordas, because, although it is not annotated, it contains all the essential supporting material including the relevant chapters from Vigny's novel *Stello*. The school texts will give additional help to anyone studying the play for examination purposes, but I have tried to offer an analysis of *Chatterton* which will also appeal to students at universities and polytechnics who may be studying it in the broader context of courses on French or European drama, or nineteenth-century literature, as well as to that nebulous character known to publishers as 'the general reader'. This does not mean taking the text itself for granted; on the contrary, I hope to give a close reading of it which will suggest some of the many avenues along which it can be explored.

1. 'Cet ouvrage austère'

On 12 February 1835, at six o'clock in the evening, Alfred de Vigny waited in the wings at the Comédie Française. He noted in his journal:

> On va jouer *Chatterton*. J'écris cette note debout, je me sens très calme, convaincu que si le drame ne réussit pas, cela ne fera rien que retarder le succès inévitable des pièces spiritualistes.
>
> Il est impossible que dans six années, s'il les faut attendre, ce que j'ai voulu faire ne soit pas senti.
>
> Unité, simplicité d'action, développement continu d'une même idée. Poésie, philosophie. (*3*, p.26)

But his confidence in the ultimate fate of his work evidently covered an underlying feeling of uncertainty. He felt that what he had tried to do was new in the theatre of his time, a drama in which ideas would predominate over action and which, as he had written six years earlier in the preface to *La Maréchale d'Ancre* ('Lettre à Lord ***', 1829), would communicate the dramatist's thought to three thousand spectators with an immediacy available only in the theatre. There was little to suggest, however, that the public was eager for this new philosophical drama and, with his habitual pessimism and his belief that poetry and philosophy were the province of an élite, he must have waited in some unease to see his audience's reaction.

In February 1830, he had witnessed the celebrated 'battles' around the performances of Victor Hugo's drama *Hernani* and had himself paved the way for the acceptance of literary Romanticism in France with his adaptation of Shakespeare's *Othello* (*Le More de Venise*, 1829). *Hernani* was in fact the culmination in a series of literary disputes which, in the theatre,

meant the gradual realisation of demands for 'une littérature
adaptée aux besoins de l'époque' and a national theatre, to take
the place of the Classical tragedy established by Racine and
Corneille (and imitated by a host of lesser writers). It was felt
that French theatre, though superior to that of other cultures,
lacked works on themes from national history such as those
dealt with in the plays of Shakespeare and other foreign drama-
tists, examples of which were published in the series of *Chefs-
d'œuvre des théâtres étrangers* from 1822; and the popularity of
the historical novels of Walter Scott, imitated by a number of
young French writers, including Vigny (*Cinq-Mars*, 1826), gave
further evidence of a growth in national consciousness and the
desire to assert the achievements of French culture, especially
beside those of Britain and Germany, the nations responsible for
the defeat of 1815. So, while respecting the rules and main-
taining the verse form of Classical tragedy, Casimir Delavigne
and Népomucène Lemercier had written plays on subjects from
modern history, creating on the stage the historical tableaux
which were the favoured genre in painting.

The theoretical essays of Schlegel, de Staël, Sismondi and
others, together with Stendhal's pamphlets *Racine et
Shakespeare* (1823 and 1825) had, in the first quarter of the
century, drawn attention to the literature of Northern Europe,
showing its conventions to be different from those of French
Classical literature, but implying that they were equally valid.
Shakespeare's popularity with English audiences made it more
difficult to dismiss him as an unlettered barbarian or even as a
genius marred by defects inherent in the literature of his age:
English audiences seemed to accept quite readily Shakespeare's
sub-plots, his changes of setting, his extension of the duration of
the narrative well beyond the 'natural' time of the performance
and the insertion of scenes like the Porter's scene in *Macbeth*
where an episode of low comedy comes directly after one of
great tragic intensity.

The literate public had been able to read Shakespeare's plays
in Guizot's translations of 1821, as well as in the *Chefs-d'œuvre
des théâtres étrangers*, but there was no evidence that they would
be acceptable on the stage. Certainly, in the previous century,

there had been Diderot's bourgeois drama (and that of Sedaine
and others), which dealt with contemporary social themes; and
there was the ever-popular melodrama which attracted lower
middle-class audiences to the boulevards for plays on foul
murder, vampirism and body-snatching. The gap between this
and 'literary' drama was vast and what Hugo, Dumas and the
other young Romantics hoped to do, was to mix elements of this
popular melodrama in works of real literary value, to draw in a
public similar to that which watched Shakespeare at Covent
Garden, drawn from a wide social spectrum and educable to
enjoy poetic drama. The elements of violence were not to be
excluded: they belonged to an age that had seen the Revolution,
the Napoleonic adventure and the Restoration. Hugo's drama
was one of action, colour and poetry.

Before their first taste of it, however, the Parisian public had
the opportunity to sample Shakespeare and greeted with jeers
the first visit to France of the English players in 1822. With their
return for the season of 1827 to 1828, led by the outstanding
British actors of the day, Kemble, Kean, Macready and Harriet
Smithson, they triumphed. An audience existed, then, for a non-
Racinian drama. 'Maintenant vienne le poète! Il y a un public',
Hugo announced in his preface to *Hernani*. Vigny himself
adapted three of Shakespeare's plays (though only one was
staged) and wrote *La Maréchale d'Ancre*, a drama in the
Hugolian melodramatic style.

Temperamentally, however, he was unsuited to Hugo's
flamboyant approach. Temperamentally, it is perhaps true to
say that he was not a man of the theatre at all, as 'untheatrical' a
dramatist as he had been an 'unmilitary' army officer. The
epigraph to his prefatory essay, 'Dernière nuit de travail',
inserted in the published editions of *Chatterton*, is taken from
Hamlet: 'Ceci est la question' (p.25). It is the crux of Hamlet's
famous monologue, the best-known phrase from Shakespeare's
most reflective work, a tragedy of thought constraining action.
So *Chatterton*, 'drame de la pensée' (p.33), is also a work about
the nature of contemplative inactivity, a cry against the doctrine
of utility, asserting the values of meditation and poetry, the
monastic ideal against that of the market place. The poet

...a besoin de *ne rien faire*, pour faire quelque chose en son art. Il faut qu'il ne fasse rien d'utile et de journalier pour avoir le temps d'écouter les accords qui se forment lentement dans son âme, et que le bruit grossier d'un travail positif et régulier interrompt et fait infailliblement évanouir. (p.29)

Nothing could be further from the atmosphere of Hugo's dramas, with their *coups de théâtre*, their mixture of the grotesque and the sublime, their violence and excess. *Chatterton* is 'austère' (p.25), its plot as simple as can be — 's'il existait une intrigue moins compliquée que celle-ci, je la choisirais' (pp.33-34) — residing essentially in the sufferings of the poet and the vain efforts of his few friends who have to watch powerless as he struggles against a hostile world.

A play, too, in prose, about poets and poetry, addressed to a French audience in 1835 but set in the house of an English industrialist in 1770. Vigny, translator of Shakespeare, well-acquainted with English literature, married to an Englishwoman, found in England the same point of reference as Hugo in Spain or Stendhal in Italy. He knew it as the birthplace of Byron and the birthplace of industrialism. His awareness of England is not irrelevant, nor is it confined to the influence of Shakespeare on a play which, for all its 'austerity' of plot, makes reference to a complex network of ideas and themes which were being discussed by Vigny's contemporaries. Despite the changes in taste in both poetry and drama, it is this concentrated treatment of important ideas, in a play remarkable for its density of structure and restraint of language, that makes *Chatterton* the most intelligent and, in the opinion of many critics, the finest work of the French Romantic theatre.

2. 'Fier, irritable et pauvre'

When the play was written, the figure of Chatterton was not new either in literature or in the work of Vigny. Shelley had included him with Sidney and Lucan among 'the inheritors of unfulfilled renown' (*Adonais*, XLV); Keats, who greatly admired him, called him 'a half-blown flower which cold blasts amate', now elevated above 'the ingrate world' ('To Chatterton', 1815) — his use of the archaic word *amate* ('subdue') making a tribute to the influence of Chatterton's medievalism; Coleridge, in his 'Monody on the Death of Chatterton', spoke of the 'Neglect and grinning scorn and Want combin'd' that had driven the earlier poet to his death; and Wordsworth, coining the most enduring phrase to express his wonder at Chatterton's precocious talent, thought of 'the marvellous Boy / The sleepless Soul that perished in his pride' (*Resolution and Independence*, VII).

So, even before the end of the eighteenth century, a certain idea of Chatterton's significance had started to emerge, focussing on his precocity, his pride, his early death and the neglect of his genius. It was an idea that appealed particularly to other poets, to the English Romantics and to young French writers who were in touch with what was happening in English literature: Vigny himself, and his friends Henri de Latouche and Charles Nodier. Latouche wrote a long poem on Chatterton's life, Nodier had been secretary to Sir Herbert Croft, a key figure in the transmission of the Chatterton story, and Vigny in 1832 published his novel *Stello*, a work which strangely anticipates psychoanalytic treatment, telling the story of a poet who visits the mysterious Docteur Noir to seek treatment for his melancholy. The doctor treats him by describing the sufferings of three representative poets under different forms of political régime: absolute monarchy (Laurent Gilbert), revolutionary republic (André Chénier) and constitutional monarchy (Chatterton). The book reflects Vigny's interest in the

Chatterton story, as well as his growing pessimism in the field of political ideas, after a period of involvement with the Utopian Saint-Simonist movement.

In examining the sources of both the play and the novel, C. Wesley Bird (9) lists eight probable influences on Vigny among the most noteworthy comments by French and English men of letters from the time of Chatterton's death in 1770 to the composition of *Stello*. I have mentioned Latouche and Nodier, the latter forming a direct link with Sir Herbert Croft whose romantic novel *Love and Madness* (1780) is the prime source for information about Chatterton's life. Writing ten years after the poet's death, Croft chanced to visit his lodgings in Shoreditch, spoke with people who had known Chatterton and worked his biography into the novel as an episode which came to occupy one-third of the book. However, the circumstances in which Croft published his findings, as part of an epistolary novel, were hardly conducive to a balanced or scholarly assessment — this had to wait another 150 years for E.H.W. Meyerstein to publish his definitive *Life* (*18*). What was available to Vigny and his contemporaries were a few facts about an obscure writer, heavily overladen with interpretation.

The facts are worth summarising, because they allow us to judge what it was about Chatterton that so strongly attracted Vigny and his contemporaries, and because we can also see how, in some instances, Vigny deliberately heightened or falsified them to make them more consistent with the image he was trying to put across. Thomas Chatterton (1753-1770) was the post-humous son of a Bristol schoolmaster. Brought up in the shadow of the lovely church of St Mary Redcliffe (still a place of pilgrimage for his admirers, and well worth visiting for its own sake), he was a late developer who learned to read, so it is said, from a black-letter Bible and became enthralled by the atmo-sphere of antiquities, old manuscripts and Gothic architecture in the church where his uncle was sexton and where he would spend hours in solitary thought. He attended a charity school which prepared poor children for apprenticeships to local trades, but left at the age of fourteen to become indentured to an attorney. The work was boring and he already had ambitions to become a poet. His first poem had been published in a local paper when he was ten, and his talent and ambition rebelled against the drudgery of the Bristol attorney's office.

The year 1768 saw the inauguration of the New Bridge in Bristol and the start of Chatterton's career as a literary forger. He sent to *Felix Farley's Journal*, a leading local newspaper, what he claimed was the transcript of a description in Middle English of the opening of the Old Bridge, which he said he had found among some parchments taken by his father from the Muniments Room at St Mary Redcliffe. There certainly were medieval manuscripts to be found in Chatterton's home: he had saved some which were being used to light the fire. But while Chatterton's family, and the authorities at St Mary Redcliffe, laid little store by old parchments, there was a growing taste for medieval antiquities, 'Gothick' ruins and haunted dungeons elsewhere in the country, and scholars had begun the study and publication of old texts, though their knowledge of Middle English was not proof against deception. A local antiquarian, excited by Chatterton's 'transcript' and by the possibility of an undiscovered hoard of manuscripts, began to make further enquiries and for him, as for the others who followed, Chatterton dutifully produced a few fragments of original material and an apparently limitless supply of 'transcripts'. The latter consisted increasingly of poems allegedly composed by a fifteenth-century monk called Rowley; some of them Chatterton had apparently written much earlier for fun, with no idea of passing them off as genuine medieval works. Once started on his deception he must have continued through sheer pleasure in the exercise of his talent, delight in fooling provincial scholars and comfort in being able to escape from the dreary attorney's office to a medieval world of his imagination.

Literary forgery was not, in any case, an unprecedented or altogether unrespectable misdemeanour. The Scotsman James Macpherson had set out to compensate for the absence of any Northern epic to rival Homer and Virgil, by collecting fragments of Gaelic oral poetry, adding material of his own, and 'translating' the whole as the works of Ossian (1765), which became immensely popular in both Britain and France. Horace Walpole, to whom Chatterton later turned for help, had appealed to a similar taste for the exotic with *The Castle of Otranto* (1764), claiming to have translated it from an Italian book of the sixteenth century. Walpole was an eminent and respected author, and this kind of literary deception was reckoned to be a legitimate ploy.

Early in 1769, Chatterton wrote to Walpole with the offer of some manuscripts, hoping to find a rich patron. The first reply was encouraging, but on receiving further samples of Rowley's work Walpole became suspicious and consulted his friend Thomas Grey. Grey was more expert than Walpole and at once suspected a hoax. Finding out that Chatterton was not, as he had imagined, an antiquarian, but simply an adolescent attorney's clerk, Walpole broke off the correspondence. It was a decision he lived to regret, for after Chatterton's death, he was blamed for not recognising the boy's talent and supporting him. Perhaps one might blame him today for his snobbish attitude to Chatterton's social status, but little else.

Chatterton was certainly very disappointed at the failure of his approach to Walpole and made up his mind to leave Bristol as soon as possible to seek fame in the literary world of London. He managed to get his release from his indentures (his employer was probably not sorry to see him go, as he had never been cut out for a life in the legal profession) and in April 1770 took lodgings in Shoreditch, determined to make his name in the fashionable press.

It is at this point that his life begins most obviously to part company with the legend. While it is true from all accounts that he was proud, even hypersensitive, he was prepared to find any work available to him in Grub Street. He poured out poetry, articles and sketches in modern English and these works, satirical, sometimes licentious but seldom remarkable among the other ephemeral literature of the time, are interesting mainly because they were written by the author of the Rowley poems, a seventeen-year-old adolescent with little formal education. Among them was a flattering epistle to the Lord Mayor, Lord Beckford, who unfortunately died before a sequel could be published. Contrary to the impression given by Vigny, Beckford was a cultured man and Chatterton was prepared to indulge in some quite obsequious praise for his stand against the King over Wilkes' expulsion from Parliament. He called on the Lord Mayor, was promised support for another poem. Chatterton was said to have been in despair on hearing of Beckford's death, and if the Lord Mayor can be in any way blamed for the poet's suicide, it is only because he chose to die at such an inconvenient time.

In the summer of 1770 Chatterton moved to Holborn, then a notoriously disreputable district. He probably needed to save money: he had not been paid for some of his published contributions to newspapers and life on the proceeds of hack journalism was precarious. He was perhaps too proud to ask for help or to admit that he needed it and Vigny may have known the report that his landlady had offered him food which he refused. It is possible, too, that he was suffering from venereal disease, in which case he would have suffered still more from the excruciating treatments prescribed at the time. During the night of August 23-24, he took arsenic and died in terrible pain, three months short of his eighteenth birthday. He may also have used opium to deaden the effects.

Once Chatterton's remains had been put in their pauper's coffin into the now-vanished Shoe Lane cemetery, interest in him centered on the problem of his authorship of the Rowley poems. Modern scholarship has established once and for all that his 'transcripts' were forgeries (if nothing else, the language, with its misinterpretation of certain Middle English words, would give the game away). But in the eighteenth century, at a time when medieval man was thought to have experienced the 'childhood' of European civilisation, naivety of style and the childish calligraphy of the manuscripts, were consistent with expectations, while social prejudice made it seem incredible that an 'untutored' youth, with neither breeding or education, could have fooled even the amateur scholars of Bristol.

Some opponents of Chatterton's authorship were to be found even in the nineteenth century, but for most people the controversy had been settled by the 1780s and the publication of *Love and Madness* directed attention away from it and towards the life of the poet and the matter of responsibility for his suicide. Most of all, his extreme youth, the precocity of his talent, the pathos of his death and his passion for the Middle Ages, appealed to the Romantic poets; and, with the exception of Wordsworth, those quoted at the start of this chapter clearly see him not only as a poet of outstanding talent (Keats, in a letter, called him 'the purest writer in the English language'), but also as an example of genius destroyed by a hostile and uncomprehending world.

The modern reader can judge Chatterton's talent for himself in modern re-editions (*11*, *12*), or at least sample the flavour of it in most anthologies of the period which include the 'Minstrel's Song' from *Aella*. As far as we are concerned, the value of Chatterton's poetry is not the issue. Whatever his place in a critical history of English literature, there can be no doubt of his extraordinary talent and the waste represented by his suicide. What matters to us is the question of how far his death was attributable to poverty and neglect and, if this was wholly or mainly the case, whether it could have been avoided. Even before Vigny, most commentators saw these as the chief factors in the suicide and Bird's study of Vigny's sources (*9*), shows both the distortion of the Chatterton legend and the process of its elevation to a myth. In this context, it is interesting to look at two accounts not cited by Bird, and possibly not known to Vigny, but which give very clear evidence of what was felt to be the poet's significance in relation to the literature and the society of his time.

The first is the article 'Chatterton' published in the *Biographie nouvelle des contemporains* (Tome IV, pp.357-59), a biographical directory which appeared in Paris in 1821. It starts by claiming that the Rowley poems show 'une harmonie sauvage...un intérêt vif, une imagination forte' which set them well above the works of Spenser and Chaucer (twice mis-spelled 'Chancer'). The poet himself is described as 'un génie d'ordre très-élevé' and 'fier, irritable et pauvre'. It gives his age at death as twenty-one and says that he spent two years in London before poisoning himself, after appealing for help to men of letters and other notables.

What is interesting here is not the inflated assessment of Chatterton's literary work or the inaccuracies about his age, but the use of the adjectives 'fier' and 'irritable' to describe his character. They reappear, also in 1821, in the article on English poetry which Philarète Chasles published in the *Revue encyclopédique* (Tome IX, p.240). He says of Chatterton that:

> ...sans amis à Londres,...en butte à l'avidité des libraires, à l'envie des gens de lettres, à la méchanceté des hommes; irritable et ardent, profond dans tous ses sentiments, fier dans sa pauvreté, naturellement mélancolique, il méprise le monde où son génie et sa jeunesse ne servent qu'à son malheur, et se donne la mort.

There is hardly a word in this brief account, by a well-informed critic, which could not be applied to the character of Chatterton in Vigny's play and, whether or not Vigny had read either of these two pieces, it has an immediate relevance to *Stello* and *Chatterton* since it indicates how, as early as the 1820s, the poet's image had become sharpened to that of a young genius, innately melancholic and susceptible, confronted by a world where youth and talent led not to recognition, but to misery and self-destruction.

Georges Lamoine (*17*) states that the reality of Chatterton's life, even that which might have been available otherwise, had become so distorted by Vigny's time that misrepresentation was inevitable. This may be true but it does not explain the three major departures from history which Vigny consciously introduced. The first is the character of Lord Beckford who appears in both the play and the novel as a coarse, opinionated and fatuous representative of the commercial bourgeoisie. The second is the character of Kitty Bell, entirely invented to supply romantic interest: in the novel, she provides the link which allows the Docteur Noir to learn Chatterton's story, so she has a functional role as well and a quite different one from that she occupies in the play, as we shall see in the following chapters (I mention her here because she is not only an invention, like John Bell or the Quaker, but because she contradicts the evidence of

Chatterton's London poems and takes so important a part in
Vigny's work that this reflects on his picture of Chatterton).
Finally, there is the insistence on Chatterton's friendship with
Lord Talbot (in the play, though not in *Stello*) and his
acquisition of a father who, instead of a provincial schoolmaster, becomes a 'bon vieux marin' (p.81). Moreover, the
friendship with Lord Talbot is extended to provide Chatterton
with an Oxford education (p.65). Why? Talbot and the other
young lords certainly contribute something to the structure of
the play and show another element of English society; their
presence is explained if Chatterton has studied with them. But
the endowment of his hero with a sailor for a father also reflects
Vigny's own ancestry and his preoccupation with military life,
and the matter of his social origin, as I suggest in Chapter 5, may
tell us something about Vigny's political and ideological stance.
At the very least, this social up-grading of Chatterton suggests
that Alfred-Victor de Vigny, heir to a noble family ruined by the
Revolution, was coming to identify with humble Tom
Chatterton in an aristocratic communion of poets.

Stello appeared in three separate parts in *La Revue des deux
mondes* in October and December 1831 and in April 1832,
before being published in book form in April 1832. Long
reviews did appear in some papers, often critical of Vigny's
political stand: in this respect, as it is hostile to all political
régimes, *Stello* was unlikely to appeal to any faction.

At first, Vigny's only intention for a sequel was a further
dialogue between Stello and the Docteur Noir. But in 1831, he
had begun an affair with the actress Marie Dorval and in 1834 he
was looking for the subject of a play which would allow her to
appear at the Théâtre Français. The Chatterton episode from
Stello gave him the opportunity to reflect on suicide and on the
fate of poets under a monarchical régime similar to that introduced in France by the July Revolution in 1830, while at the
same time providing, in Kitty Bell, an attractive female lead.

The play was written, he tells us in the 'Dernière nuit de
travail' (p.25), in seventeen nights during June 1834. At first,
because of hostility to Dorval, the Théâtre Français refused it
and when eventually, after the intervention of the Queen and the

Duc d'Orléans, it was accepted, rehearsals immediately ran into difficulties. Joanny (the Quaker) was distracted because of the recent death of his father, Geffroy (Chatterton) did not get on with Marie Dorval and, as his notes in the *Journal d'un poète* show, Vigny had mixed feelings about his leading actor. At last, the difficulties were overcome and the play opened in February 1835.

Because he planned the play for Marie Dorval, Vigny's first consideration in writing it was to heighten the character of Kitty Bell and make her love for Chatterton a major theme in the drama. In *Stello*, on the other hand, she plays essentially the role of an intermediary between Chatterton and the Docteur Noir who learns of Chatterton's story largely in the form of his letter to Kitty (pp.121-24). Her gradual realisation of her feelings on the stage becomes a powerful focus of dramatic interest. Most of the other alterations have the effect of illuminating her character and that of Chatterton: the scene with the young aristocrats, for example, or the transformation of her husband from the humble saddler of the novel to the powerful industrialist shown in the play (which also allows Vigny to comment more fully on the position of women in a male-dominated society). Apart from this, he is mainly concerned to tighten up the dialogue and the action, making them more suited for a stage drama: the way he does this might be studied in a comparison of the scene with Lord Beckford (pp.94-99) with the corresponding scene in *Stello* (pp.132-39).

In the play, the Docteur Noir vanishes to be replaced by the Quaker (adding some of the local colour lost when Kitty becomes a housewife rather than the keeper of a pie-shop). Now that Kitty is unemployed, the action can be confined almost exclusively to the back room in John Bell's house and so subjected almost perfectly to the classical unities of time, place and action. The changes are not in fact trivial: they all tend towards the same concentration of the drama, the same heightening of the dramatic effect and the creation of a play which realises the image so vividly evoked in the 'Dernière nuit de travail' (p.31): that of a circle of fire inside which the scorpion is trapped, turns helplessly and finally meets its death.

3. 'Martyrs et bourreaux'

The Docteur Noir and Stello represent two divergent human types as well as personifying what Vigny saw as the conflicting aspects of his own nature. On the one hand there is the stoical rationalist, distanced from life, who coldly analyses the human condition; on the other, the poet, passionately involved, his enthusiasms and imaginative sympathies refusing to let him accept as inevitable either his own misfortunes or those of others. Personal conflicts and disappointments (his mother's illness, his liaison with Marie Dorval, his growing disillusionment in the political sphere), contributed to intensify his unease during the early 1830s and are reflected in the mood of the novel. As far as politics are concerned, his cynicism may be dated from the time of the July 1830 Revolution, and is evident in all three episodes of *Stello*; but the last (André Chénier) is noticeably more detached than the first two (Gilbert and Chatterton), suggesting that even as he wrote the novel, he was experiencing a crystallization around the idea that nothing was to be expected from any form of régime. This is carried over into the play, together with an alienation from orthodox religion and a preoccupation with suicide: 'les stoïciens l'appelaient *sortie raisonnable*', Chatterton says (p.83).

This sombre mood colours the play, not least in the physical appearance of the main characters, as indicated in the author's notes (pp.35-37). Chatterton wears a black coat and jacket with grey trousers; Kitty Bell, a black hat, grey silk dress and black ribbons; John Bell, a brown coat; the Quaker, brown or grey coat, jacket, breeches and stockings. 'J'avais désiré,' Vigny explains, 'et j'avais obtenu que cet ensemble offrît l'aspect sévère et simple d'un tableau flamand' (p.109). Against this setting of blacks, browns and greys, the aristocrats erupt in their rich costumes, their insouciance clashing visibly with the sobriety of John Bell's household. There could be no clearer indication of the inability of Lord Beckford and Lord Talbot to understand or intervene effectively on behalf of those who are imprisoned in this bleak atmosphere of repression, misunderstanding and impending disaster.

While the variegated dress of the intruders (Beckford, Talbot and the other lords) expresses the same aura of wealth, power and self-assurance, the harmonising colours worn by the central characters indicate something different in each case. John Bell's dress is utilitarian, appropriate to a man in the middle ranks of society engaged in the management of men and affairs. The Quaker dresses in accordance with the gravity of his disposition and the sobriety of his sect, while Kitty demonstrates her modesty and self-effacement. The bourgeois interior may suit the style of these three to a greater or lesser extent, but it stifles Chatterton whose clothes are dictated by his desire for anonymity and by his poverty; poets in Vigny's day inclined to flamboyance and dandyism when they could afford it.

It is the Quaker who divides mankind into two groups, *martyrs* and *bourreaux* (p.50). Taken literally, these categories are quite appropriate to Chatterton and to John Bell: there is a sense in which Chatterton does indeed die as a witness to his faith and John Bell readily accepts his role as torturer or executioner, referring, as the Quaker says, to the fact that it is sanctioned by the law (p.43). But John Bell, though self-righteous and consciously inhuman in his treatment of his workers, is unaware of the sufferings he inflicts on Kitty. What really distinguishes the *martyrs* from the *bourreaux* in a more general sense, is sensitivity. The pain of the *martyrs* is intensified by their ability to feel in themselves and for others, the quality which Vigny describes as *cœur* or *âme*. It is this that enrols the Quaker among them, but at the same time explains the delicacy of feeling which prevents him from intervening effectively to help Chatterton and Kitty and restrains the two lovers from expressing their love. It is above all the lack of sensitivity which makes the *bourreaux*: Beckford and Talbot are well-meaning, but callous; they enjoy the thrill of the hunt, without actually taking a sadistic pleasure in the suffering of the fox. One might even extend this to say that it is their insensitivity that makes them ready to accept the world as it is and, more than self-interest, dictates their political beliefs. Vigny insists that a characteristic of the poet is his ability to feel sympathy for others: 'ceux qu'il plaint souffrent moins que lui, et il se meurt des peines des autres' (p.28).

The Quaker

It is almost inevitable that one should turn first to the Quaker among the characters in the play, because of the way in which he is allowed partly to take over the function of the Docteur Noir, in *Stello*, as narrator and interpreter of the action and the characters. He is the head, not the heart, in this 'drame de la pensée', though his dispassionate analysis of events does not tempt us to ask, as Stello does of the Docteur Noir: 'Hélas! ...êtes-vous né sans entrailles?' (7, p.37). There is, however, a contradiction between his role as 'chorus' and his participation as a character on stage.

If he is both more sympathetic and less mysterious than the Docteur Noir, it is because he is defined as a member of a religious sect which was both foreign and familiar to a French audience. The Society of Friends was founded in the seventeenth century, by George Fox, and its members, who early accepted the name 'Quakers', were distinguished by their sobriety and their refusal to accept any authority in temporal or spiritual matters. In contrast to the orthodoxy imposed on Catholic France, the Quakers were tolerated in Britain after 1689 and this liberal attitude towards religious dissidence was a feature of English life which particularly interested French writers. Voltaire, in the *Lettres philosophiques* (1734), devotes four chapters to the Quakers and, in particular, describes a meeting with a Quaker who bears a strong resemblance to the character in Vigny's play. An old man, wearing 'un grand chapeau à bords rabattus', he impresses Voltaire with his benevolence, his sobriety and the absence of affectation in his manners. They eat a frugal meal together and Voltaire, mainly concerned with implying an oblique and ironical comment on Catholic dogma, pretends to ridicule his commonsense attitude to religious questions. Despite some good-humoured amusement at the more eccentric features of Quaker dress and behaviour, Voltaire's account is sympathetic and it would have been known to Vigny and to many members of his audience.

Two other features of Quaker usage were well-known in France from Voltaire's letters and other sources: these were the Quakers' refusal to take oaths (p.59), and their indiscriminate use of the second person singular (in English the forms *thee* and *thou*), reflecting their belief that all men are equal in the sight of God and that one should avoid 'polite' forms of address which would imply that one was too much a 'respecter of persons'. The Quaker is consequently the only character in the play to use the *tu* form in conversation with others, except for the one instance of Chatterton addressing Kitty as *tu* in his final words to her (p.105), this anomaly clearly showing the strength of his feeling and the significance of the moment. Otherwise, Chatterton does use the *tu* form in his monologue (pp.79-82), while the Quaker once addresses Kitty as *vous* (p.76), this change to the second person plural, like his earlier use of the title 'madame', indicating his momentary annoyance with her — as Kitty realises when she exclaims: 'Madame? - Ah! ne vous fâchez pas.' (p.76).

As well as being an accurate reflection of Quaker usage in English, this restriction of the *tu* form to the Quaker's speech in the play also gives him a peculiar intimacy with the other characters and confirms his central role as 'chorus' (like the chorus in a Greek tragedy whose members also have the habit of addressing the characters directly). His benevolent attitude to all men is consistent with his religious belief, but also emphasises the distance between him and the active participants in the drama; at times, he appears in relation to them almost like an author observing the characters he has created. In purely human terms, his benevolence would be either hypocritical or frankly implausible; only someone divorced from the action could say to John Bell: 'j'ai pour toi une amitié véritable' (p.46).

The sentence just quoted is a relatively rare example of the use by the Quaker of the first person singular. Not only is he identified by his use of the *tu* form, but as commentator he speaks about others rather than about himself. It is he who

identifies the characters for us: John Bell, 'une espèce de
vautour qui écrase sa couvée' (p.43), Kitty, 'âme simple et tour-
mentée' (p.42), and so on. In the same way, his speech is sometimes tediously aphoristic; he tends towards such generalisations
as: 'Il n'y a pas de sagesse humaine' (p.42) or 'un silence qui
vient de l'orgueil peut être mal compris' (p.71) and employs such
rhetorical devices as oxymoron ('vice presque vertueux, noble
imperfection, péché sublime', p.77) and antithesis ('ils aiment
assez à faire vivre les morts et mourir les vivants', p.53). His use
of language has a distancing effect, setting him apart from what
is happening on stage, as does his fondness for the dramatic
device of the aside addressed directly to the audience ('toutes les
routes le ramènent à son idée fixe', p.84; 'la mère donne à ses
enfants un baiser d'amante sans le savoir', p.95). Even when he
is ostensibly directing his remarks to one of the other characters,
they are in the nature of such asides, as when he tells Rachel:
'...tu passeras ta vie d'esclave...' (p.49).

As well as distinguishing *martyrs* from *bourreaux*, the Quaker
also makes most frequent use of the words *cœur* (twelve times)
and *âme* (seven times) by which Vigny designates the qualities of
sensitivity and feeling peculiar to the *martyrs*. In particular, he
contrasts *cœur* and *esprit* in Chatterton (p.50), stressing the
distinction between emotion and reason which is a guiding
theme of both *Stello* and the play. Similarly, it is by reference to
this quality of *cœur* that he qualifies both the *martyr* Chatterton
and the *bourreau* John Bell, saying of the latter 'ton cœur est
d'acier comme tes mécaniques' (p.47), and of the former 'ton
cœur est pur et jeune comme celui de Rachel' (p.50), the parallel
between the two similes underlining their effect.

The same qualities of purity and childlike simplicity are those
which the Quaker recognises in Kitty ('Vous allez dire à votre
bonne petite mère que son cœur est simple, pur et véritablement
chrétien; mais qu'elle est plus enfant que vous dans sa conduite',
he says, speaking to the children, p.42); and this definition of
the two lovers, as well as explaining the affinity between them,
refers to a characteristic of poets, in Vigny's view, to which I
shall return in Chapter 5. 'Pauvre enfant!' (p.50), he says to
Chatterton (who replies: 'Pauvre? oui. — Enfant? non...j'ai

vécu mille ans!'), later describing him to Kitty as one of those 'âmes jeunes, ardentes et toutes neuves à la vie' (p.76). Chatterton describes himself as 'inoffensif comme les enfants' (p.62) and this particular image of the poet as simple and child-like gives rise to a series of epithets which come to have a special significance within the play, as they did elsewhere in Vigny's work: *sauvage, primitif, simple, naïf*, because they identified for him the qualities of the poetic spirit which make it unacceptable to a utilitarian, bourgeois society. Perhaps it is no accident that John Bell should exclaim: 'les enfants sont désœuvrés, je n'aime pas cela' (p.48) — a simple aside, but one completely in character and consistent with the inability of men like Bell and Beckford to accept the 'idleness' essential to the poet. The Quaker, though not a poet and not childlike ('je suis très vieux', p.85), is identified as belonging to the ranks of the *martyrs* not only by his ability to understand them, but also when Talbot picks on him as 'cet animal sauvage' and instantly makes him an object of persecution: 'Oh! quel bonheur! un quaker!... c'est un gibier que nous n'avions pas fait lever encore' (p.66). Wild animals are 'fair game' because they refuse to conform to the norms of a society which seeks to domesticate them. Thus the Quaker calls Chatterton 'fort sauvage' (p.87), the same word being applied to him also by Talbot (p.65) and to Kitty by John Bell (p.65), the husband thus unconsciously touching on one of the qualities which make for the affinity between Kitty and Chatterton when he adopts the term just employed by Talbot. Chatterton identifies with 'le sanglier solitaire' (p.62), the off-stage noises of the chase being suggestive for an audience in France where the wild boar is still hunted. For Vigny, the significant characteristic of wild animals is that they are mute victims of men's sport and not tamed to the ritual cruelty of society: hence the similarity with children and poets whose 'cœurs jeunes, simples et primitifs ne savent pas encore étouffer les vives indignations que donne la vue des hommes' (p.68). In this, and the references to hunting, Vigny anticipates the poems of *Les Destinées*, in particular 'La Mort du loup', the conclusion of which is summed up in the Quaker's stoical remark: 'il faut vivre, te taire et prier Dieu!' (p.86).

It might seem that I have drifted some way from consideration of the character of the Quaker, but in fact his primary role in the play is to be found in just this function as the definer and most frequent user of these key words which take on a unique colouring within the linguistic context of the work. The word *martyr*, for example, which he first uses (p.50), is picked up again by Chatterton when he says 'une torture de plus dans un martyre, qu'importe' (p.71), returning to the Quaker again in the last line of the play: 'dans ton sein, Seigneur, reçois ces deux martyrs' (p.106). Similarly, references to suicide, to sickness and health, to destiny, as well as the highly suggestive terms quoted in the last two paragraphs, though they are not reserved exclusively for the Quaker, form a network of concepts which he chiefly defines and on which he comments as the drama unfolds.

A dramatic character who has to carry so much of the play-wright's own commentary, is bound to suffer from some lack of plausibility. Vigny does his best to counteract this, firstly by stressing the Quaker's exceptional wisdom and virtue, respected by all the other characters, and secondly by giving quite detailed explanations of his presence in John Bell's house (p.46), as well as letting the Quaker himself in one of his few personal statements, describe some of his background (p.85). The fact that he is a doctor provides a link with the Docteur Noir, an explanation of his relationship with John Bell and an association with the ideas of sickness and health running through the play. Even John Bell, who is supposed to feel gratitude to him for saving the life of one of his children (p.46), describes him as an exceptional member of a sect which is itself an exception in the Christian world (p.45), Talbot calls him 'bon Quaker' (p.89), after a change of heart, while Kitty and Chatterton make frequent reference to his fairness and objectivity, in particular Chatterton when he calls him 'mon sévère ami' (to which the Quaker responds by stressing the limitations of his power to console and heal) and Kitty, in the most complete and precise definition of his role in the dramatic scheme of the play, when she says:

Vous êtes au-dessus de nous tous par votre prudence; vous
pourriez voir à vos pieds tous nos petits orages que vous
méprisez, et cependant, sans être atteint, vous y prenez
part; vous en souffrez par indulgence, et puis vous laissez
tomber quelques mots, et les nuages se dissipent, et nous
vous rendons grâces, et les larmes s'effacent, et nous
sourions, parce que vous l'avez permis. (p.88)

This highly idealised character would have been somewhat
easier for a French audience to accept because he belongs to the
religious sect known from Voltaire's *Lettres philosophiques*
(where the figure of the Quaker is also idealised, though for
rather different reasons), to be outstanding in its rectitude and
austerity: 'nos assemblées religieuses, où l'on ne voit pas
l'agitation des papistes, adorateurs d'images, où l'on n'entend
pas les chants puérils des protestants...' (p.52). His obedience to
his conscience and his scrupulosity ('si j'avais raison au fond,
j'ai eu tort dans la forme', pp.42-43), as well as contributing to
the impression of him as an exception even among Quakers,
contrasts with the *bourreaux* who are just and reasonable
according to human, not divine, law.

It is hard, even so, to accept his protestation of friendship for
John Bell and his non-involvement in the action when he can see
the direction of Chatterton's thoughts and the danger of Kitty's
affection for the poet. His non-involvement is not, in fact,
complete: he does refuse to leave the room when John Bell asks
him to do so (p.68), because he does not want Kitty and
Chatterton to be left alone; and he attempts to prevent
Chatterton's suicide by appealing to his desire for fame (p.84)
and by revealing Kitty's feelings for him (p.85). Of course, we
know that these pleas will not succeed and they serve chiefly to
create suspense by delaying an outcome we know to be
inevitable. Despite them, and despite his role as intermediary
between Kitty and Chatterton in the stilted second scene of Act
II, he remains essentially the vehicle for Vigny's own comment
and a foil for Chatterton's passionate nature.

Chatterton

When one takes the figure of an historical poet and sets out to depict through him The Poet, something has got to give. Vigny makes his position quite clear:

Le Poète était tout pour moi: Chatterton n'était qu'un nom d'homme, et je viens d'écarter à dessein des faits exacts de sa vie pour ne prendre de sa destinée que ce qui la rend un exemple à jamais déplorable d'une noble misère. (p.34)

though this defence begs the question of whether a fictional account *can* be a valid example of *une noble misère*, if the reality was not thought sufficiently exemplary in itself; and the changes which Vigny makes to the biography of the poet, as it was known in his time, such as the attribution to him of a university education and a fictitious father, seem to add nothing to the exemplary quality of his life.

To the alterations to the known biography mentioned in the last chapter, I will add two, from Chatterton's monologue: firstly, the poem *The Battle of Hastings* was written before the poet came to London; secondly, the critics Miles and Warton (p.81) did not publish their doubts on his authorship of the Rowley poems until after his death. Both of these changes, however, may be justified within the context of Vigny's play, the first because it quotes a typical work by Chatterton of the Rowley period, the second because it serves to personify attacks that were actually made on his poetry. For the rest, it is probably better from now on to treat the character in the play as purely fictional and to forget the real Chatterton, considering the dramatic character rather as an amalgam of ideas on poetry and poets which belong to Vigny's time more than to the previous century.

Vigny concludes his novel by defining Stello as 'le sentiment' and the Docteur Noir as 'le raisonnement' and the same pair are represented in the play by the Quaker and Chatterton, though Chatterton in particular is developed to signify much more than simply this division between heart and head, feeling and contemplation. The contrast itself emerges most clearly in the speech of the two characters. Where the Quaker, using the *tu* form as more than just the badge of his sect, speaks about others or encapsulates his experience and his stoical resignation in sententious remarks, Chatterton, more than any other character in the play, is wedded to the use of the first person singular, his over-riding concern the typically Romantic one of discovering and dramatising his own personality:

> Pour moi, j'ai résolu de ne me point masquer et d'être moi-même jusqu'à la fin, d'écouter, en tout, mon cœur dans ses épanchements comme dans ses indignations, et de me résigner à bien accomplir ma loi...On me trahit de tout côté, je le vois, et me laisse tromper par dédain de moi-même, par ennui de prendre ma défense... (p.51)

A third 'law' is thus added to the political law used by John Bell and Beckford to justify their exploitation of others, and the divine law (or that of his conscience) respected by the Quaker: the law dictated to Chatterton by his own nature, an inner necessity imposing a particular course of action with the inevitability of fate.

Even in his occasional axiomatic remark, Chatterton particularises, relating his generalisation sardonically to his own case:

> La bonté d'un homme ne le rend victime que jusqu'où il le veut bien, et l'affranchissement est dans sa main. (p.50)

This clearly recalls Hamlet's soliloquy (directly quoted in the epigraph to the 'Dernière nuit de travail', p.25):

> For who would bear the whips and scorns of time...
> When he himself might his quietus make
> With a bare bodkin?   (III, 1)

And Hamlet is one of the sources of a character of whom the

Quaker remarks: 'En toi, la rêverie continuelle a tué l'action' (p.51); most obviously in the theme of suicide, but also in Chatterton's monologue where the address to his father echoes Hamlet's meetings with his father's ghost (and may explain why Chatterton's father has become an old man in the play), as well as the suggestion of madness as Chatterton utters his 'stream of consciousness', but a 'madness' that, like Hamlet's, serves, behind the apparently random juxtapositioning of ideas, to reveal his train of thought.

Hamlet's indecision — the contemplative man, in opposition to the man of action — and the sense that he is driven by a fatality outside himself, appealed to the Romantics and explain the oblique references to Shakespeare in Vigny's play. Hamlet's madness, too, is consistent with the idea of genius bordering on insanity and sickness: Goethe defined Romanticism as sickness, Classicism as health, and the theme of genius as an infliction runs through Vigny's play, from the moment when the Quaker exclaims: 'La maladie est incurable!' (p.54), through Chatterton's reference to 'la contagion de mon infortune' (p.62), to his final moments when he says: 'Je suis guéri' (p.102). The disease is contagious in that the sufferer (like that other Romantic hero, Hernani, in Victor Hugo's play) brings misfortune on all around him; it is also unavoidable and incurable — hence the *caractère fatal* of poetic genius (p.52) — and leads to the poet's isolation from his fellow-men.

In Chapter 5, I shall try to examine some of the reasons for this particular view of poetic genius and the elements in Chatterton's character which help to make him the epitome of the Romantic poet. It may be, however, that the most telling aspect of his personality and the one that identifies him most clearly as a figure from the nineteenth, rather than any previous century, is the mania for introspection that allows him to discover his own nature and what distinguishes him from the rest of mankind. It is partly, as has often been said, that Classical writers sought to depict general types, in contrast to the Romantic obsession with the individual; but the difference is really that between those elements in the human personality which engage man with his fellows, as a social animal, and the

ultimate inner loneliness of the individual, which explains the
Romantic interest in one particular type, that of the 'outsider'
(to use a word applied by a later generation) in whom the
isolation of the individual is most evident and can be most
clearly depicted. Chatterton, too, is a type, his universal
character most obvious to us in the way in which Vigny draws on
a range of different sources in creating him and in the expressed
intention of revealing general truths about poetry and poets.

Chatterton's introspection leads him to a character which
contains a number of contradictory elements. Some of these
contradictions are authentic, some only apparent, and some
(though Vigny surely does not intend us to see them as such)
deriving from what may appear now to be the striking of poses.
This impression comes from our comparison with the models on
which Vigny, consciously or unconsciously, drew for the central
character in his play (and perhaps the modern reader's
involuntary assumption that Chatterton himself knew these
models and was copying them), but they are more than just an
indication that the character is an amalgam of Shakespearean,
Byronic and other influences. An element of contradiction is
inherent in the Romantic view of the human personality. While
the Classical writer would see the personality as more or less
static, imposed by Nature and human nature and apparent from
the individual's behaviour in social situations, the Romantic
view was essentially dynamic. It depicted the human drama less
as the outcome of a struggle between human desires and external
pressures (Phèdre's guilty love for her stepson in Racine's play
or the conflict between passion and honour in Corneille's *Le
Cid*), than as an irreconcilable struggle within the individual in
which his own nature or identity becomes the central dramatic
issue.

In Hugo's plays these problems were often externalised in
scenes of disguise and mistaken identity such as the various
transformations of Hernani and Ruy Blas; and the 'unmasking'
of Chatterton by the arrival of the young Lords (Act II, scene 3),
which leads Kitty in the following scene to exclaim: 'Ils ont l'air
de connaître si bien monsieur Chatterton! et nous, nous le
connaissons si peu!' (p.70), is a comparable situation. The

message, as in *Ruy Blas*, is partly that nobility does not depend on titles (and only someone as shallow as John Bell could imagine that it does), an idea stressed by the dramatic irony of Kitty's remark, since the audience realises that in fact Kitty knows the 'real' Chatterton much better than the Lords, who are only superficially acquainted with him and have shown by their behaviour that they have no real understanding of his feelings. But the question of identity is more fundamental than this and revolves throughout the play around the ambiguity of Chatterton's thirst for fame and his desire for anonymity. His horror at the arrival of Lord Talbot and the others cannot be covered by the 'rational' explanation given for his presence in John Bell's house: that he is trying to escape his creditors. His fear is at the revelation of the name which he has hidden from Bell and Kitty, and from the public since he chose to publish his poems as the work of a medieval monk. His suicide is provoked finally by the success of this deception.

A name is the clearest expression of a person's identity and the desire to hide or disguise it, a form of self-destruction, denial of the self or escape from an imprisoning persona. There is a characteristically Romantic obsession with heroic anonymity, illustrated in Byron's poem *The Giaour*, which begins and ends with its hero's unmarked grave:

'Then lay me with the humblest dead,
And, save the cross above my head,
Be neither name nor emblem spread,
By prying stranger to be read,
Or stay the passing pilgrim's tread'.
He pass'd — nor of his name and race
Hath left a token or a trace... (*10*, p.172)

The name, too, is an aspect of one's identity which can be possessed by others, a feature of domestic animals as opposed to the *sauvage*, the *primitif*, the *sanglier solitaire*, a symbol of the power of society to designate and to define.

The name, with its connotations of identity, is therefore one of the central motifs of the play, introduced by Kitty's inability to denote Chatterton except as 'le jeune monsieur' (p.41) and highlighted at the start of Act II when the Quaker interprets as an act of folly Chatterton's terror of being discovered, saying that a friend is not much worse than any other kind of man:

CHATTERTON

Il ne pouvait rien m'arriver de pis que de le voir. Mon asile était violé, ma paix était troublée, mon nom était connu ici.

LE QUAKER

Le grand malheur!

CHATTERTON

Le savez-vous, mon nom, pour en juger?

LE QUAKER

Il y a quelque chose de bien puéril dans ta crainte. Tu n'es que sauvage, et tu seras pris pour un criminel si tu continues. (p.60)

Once the revelation has been made, Kitty repeatedly addresses him as 'monsieur Chatterton' (p.70), and is surprised that he should have left the social circles to which the possession of his name admits him, 'pour cacher son nom, et sa vie dans une famille aussi simple que la nôtre' (p.71); to which Chatterton replies with an emphatic defence of his real identity against the threat represented by Kitty's distancing use of his name (an indication of her alienation from him in this scene) and by the social relationships implied in it:

Si l'on m'avait demandé ici ma fortune, mon nom et l'histoire de ma vie, je n'y serais pas entré... Si quelqu'un me les demandait aujourd'hui, j'en sortirais. (p.71)

The urge to 'be oneself', or to 'find oneself' is thus intimately associated in the play with the need to escape from the constricting definitions made by society at one's birth, and before: when Chatterton is speaking to his dead father, he tells him: '...je vous assure que *votre nom* n'ira pas en prison' (p.82, emphasis added). Vigny, aware that his own name made him heir to a noble family, is aware too that Thomas Chatterton, son of a Bristol schoolmaster, is his equal by his poetic genius and, having taken this 'nom d'homme' for the hero of his drama, apologises to him:

> Ame désolée, pauvre âme de dix-huit ans! pardonne-moi de prendre pour symbole le nom que tu portais sur la terre, et de tenter le bien en ton nom. (p.34)

'Anon.' may be the author of some fine poetry, but it is not a title to which any poet aspires. Yet, as Stello remarks with irony on hearing the name of Lord Beckford:

> Et que m'importent à moi les trois ou quatre syllabes d'un nom?...Le Laocoon et le Vénus de Milo sont anonymes, et leurs statuaires ont cru leurs noms immortels en cognant leurs blocs avec un petit marteau. Le nom d'Homère, ce nom de demi-dieu, vient d'être rayé du monde par un monsieur grec! Gloire, rêve d'une ombre! a dit Pindare, s'il a existé, car on n'est sûr de personne à présent. (p.133)

The individual, however, survives in the work, sanctified by the minds and feelings of succeeding generations. The name which Chatterton is so anxious to conceal from his contemporaries, only becomes his true identity when applied to

> ...ces œuvres naïves et puissantes que créa le génie primitif et méconnu de *Chatterton, mort à dix-huit ans*! Cela ne devrait faire qu'un nom, comme *Charlemagne*, tant cela est beau, étrange, unique et grand. (p.128)

(in Stello's words). It is this that explains Chatterton's aspiration for a true glory (not the transient fame of the Lord Mayor), and his despair when he thinks that his forgery, concealing his work under Rowley's name, has denied him the credit which is his due. 'J'espérais que l'illusion de ce nom supposé ne serait qu'un voile pour moi; je sens qu'elle m'est un linceul' (p.122), he exclaims in the novel; and in the play cries out: 'mon nom est étouffé! ma gloire éteinte! mon honneur perdu!' (p.100).

His suicide, however, reverses the verdict of contemporary misunderstanding and ensures that Chatterton, far from being simply *un nom d'homme*, should attain his apotheosis as *symbole*, *merveilleux enfant* and myth. No wonder the play, for all Vigny's insistence that it should be seen as a plea for the state to remedy a situation that drove poets to despair, should have been widely condemned as encouraging suicide when Chatterton's martyrdom is so crucial to his identity.

In the end, moreover, it is the total obliteration of himself that Chatterton desires, finding freedom and equality only in death and rejoining the Byronic hero in his determination to eliminate all trace of his existence: 'Mort, Ange de délivrance, que ta paix est douce...Regarde-moi, Ange sévère, leur ôter à tous la trace de mes pas sur la terre' (p.100). This final monologue is his apotheosis ('...remontez au ciel avec moi!'), the final dramatic irony that the spectator, like Stello, realises the poet's true glory will be his epitaph: *Chatterton, mort à dix-huit ans*. Perhaps, for us, the true sense in which he merits the martyr's crown is the sense in which his posthumous destiny can only be realised by this early and voluntary death.

Chatterton, *martyr*, is irreligious, a believer in destiny, for which the Quaker, appropriately, reproaches him (p.62); and Vigny, himself a sceptic and a stoic, shared this belief in an impersonal fate, which perhaps explains why, in what may have been an unguarded moment, he puts Chatterton's word into the Quaker's mouth: 'La Fortune change souvent...' (p.83) — unless one chooses to defend the characterisation of the Quaker by saying that he is appealing to an idea which he feels may dissuade Chatterton from his intention. Yet throughout the play, one is struck by the number of metaphors directly derived from religion and particularly by those which Chatterton himself uses to describe his dedication to his art. He sees himself as a monk: 'J'ai fait de ma chambre la cellule d'un cloître; j'ai béni et sanctifié ma vie et ma pensée' (p.52), implying that this total dedication to poetry is essential to the practice of it and is imposed on him, like a vocation, from outside, by a power stronger than himself: '...j'écris. — Pourquoi? je n'en sais rien... Parce qu'il le faut' (p.54).

This elevation of art into a religion and the adoption in speaking of it of terms borrowed from religious practice, reaches its climax in the series of images in which Chatterton compares himself with Christ. 'Eh! cependant,' he asks, 'n'ai-je quelque droit à l'amour de mes frères, moi qui travaille pour eux nuit et jour...?' (p.52), stressing the physical suffering which this sacrifice entails (p.53), an idea picked up in his first monologue, where he contemplates his open heart, source of the feeling he puts into his work, exhibited like the Sacred Heart of Jesus: 'S'il a des blessures, tant mieux!' (p.79). Most directly of all, he exclaims: 'Il est écrit que je ne pourrai poser ma tête nulle part' (p.60), directly quoting Christ's word (Matthew, 8, 20): 'but the Son of Man hath not where to lay his head'.

This identification with Christ as man, rejected and betrayed, is a typically Romantic aspect of Chatterton's character, like his feeling that 'ma vie est de trop à tout le monde' (p.49), his lassitude and his statement: 'J'ai vécu mille ans!' (p.50), which recalls Byron's entry in a Swiss hotel register where he put his age as 100. There is an element of self-dramatisation in Chatterton's presentation of himself (which may be inevitable in any martyrdom consciously accepted, since martyrdom is itself an extreme way of dramatising one's position), and also of self-pity. The conscious identification with Christ serves Vigny's purpose as a continuation of the theme of obedience to human law (Bell) and divine law (the Quaker), by adding a third road: that of obedience to the dictates of art and the poetic nature. But the point is made at the expense of the character.

'Les passions des poètes n'existent qu'à peine...franchement ils n'aiment rien; ce sont tous des égoïstes...Le cerveau se nourrit au dépens du cœur' (p.101): Chatterton's generalisation is obviously designed to protect Kitty from the fatal consequences of her love for him; so too is the Quaker's similar remark that 'les auteurs n'aiment que leurs manuscrits...Il ne tient à personne, il n'aime personne' (p.87), which is to be seen in the same light as his description of Kitty as 'une jeune femme très froide, qui n'est émue que pour ses enfants, quand ils sont malades' (p.61). But in the case of Chatterton, we are more inclined to believe that there is some truth in this view of him. His self-absorption is evident from his speech; and while Kitty at the start of the play says that she would not lie even to save her children (p.55), by the end her love for Chatterton has so far replaced all other considerations with her, that she is prepared to say: 'enfin je ferai mon crime aussi, moi; je mentirai; voilà tout' (p.77). Chatterton's love for her can never possess him to the extent of displacing his art. It is Kitty who dies for love; Chatterton dies because society has rejected him and he can see no other solution consistent with his image of himself.

Kitty

The love between Kitty and Chatterton grows out of Kitty's sympathy for the young man, a sympathy which is not only akin to a feeling of pity, but also, in the framework of a play centred on the self-absorbed figure of the poet, dangerously close to a form of transferred self-pity. This impression will be proportional to the strength of the spectator's or reader's feeling of identification with the central character and his interpretation of how far the writer himself identifies with Chatterton. Even if we do not feel inclined to go to the extent of seeing Kitty as merely a projection of Vigny's/Chatterton's desire for sympathy and love, a vague unease remains about the emotion which unites the two central characters. It is a love that is never asked to confront the mature problems it raises: the question of Kitty's marriage and her children, the choice between progress and renunciation. It remains essentially an adolescent emotion, resolved by the adolescent solution of suicide.

Having said this, it is nonetheless easy to see why the love between Kitty and Chatterton is crucial to the unfolding of the drama. Kitty is the most fully realised *dramatic* character in the play, because, unlike Chatterton and the Quaker, she makes explicit to the audience emotions of which she herself is unaware and the conflicts which derive from her needs and feelings are internal to her. While both Chatterton and the Quaker, from their first appearance, announce that they stand for poetic genius or Christian charity, and prepare consciously to defend their identities against the threat of an unpoetic and uncharitable society, Kitty declares herself to be the symbol of an innocence and purity which, by its very nature, cannot anticipate the threats to which it will be exposed. In her, the childlike simplicity which characterises the *martyrs*, becomes a source of powerful dramatic tension. 'Je ne suis qu'une femme simple et faible; je ne sais que mes devoirs de chrétienne' (p.56), she says, adding: 'il n'y a pas une minute de ma vie dont le souvenir puisse me faire rougir' (p.57). Yet, only a moment later, she asks: 'Pourquoi, lorsque j'ai touché la main de mon mari, me suis-je reproché d'avoir gardé ce livre?' (p.58). Her answer, that she will return the book, is no answer to the question she has asked.

The rhetorical question shows that it is for the audience alone that she articulates her feelings, remaining herself unaware of them. It is the first of a series of such questions which she either leaves unanswered, or to which she gives similarly evasive replies. 'Hélas! il n'est donc plus malheureux? — J'en suis bien aise' (p.62), the contradiction between the exclamation and the feeling she claims to experience patently indicating the conflict between her desire to see Chatterton happy and her need to feel that he is dependent on her sympathy; 'Ah! mon Dieu! pourquoi s'est-il enfui de la sorte?...Pourquoi est-il venu ici?' (p.71), once more expressing conflicting emotions and preparing for the succession of rhetorical questions (pp.71-72) in Kitty's next speech; 'Qu'est-il venu faire ici? qu'a-t-il voulu en se faisant plaindre?' (p.74), where Vigny, with nice psychological insight, shows her trying to transfer responsibility for the threatening emotion she feels to Chatterton who has inspired it; 'J'ai envoyé mes enfants pour le distraire; et ils ont voulu absolument lui porter leur goûter, leurs fruits, que sais-je? Est-ce un grand crime à moi, mon ami? en est-ce un à mes enfants?' (p.87), as if she could share the innocence of the children. Even her final questions ('pourquoi dites-vous: J'ai été?' p.101...etc.) leave her one step behind the audience, while her ultimate declaration of her love takes the form: 'Et si je vous aime, moi!' (p.104), as she tentatively faces up to the inevitable implications of their situation.

This constant interrogation of herself and the unanswered questions she addresses to the other characters, involve the audience directly in Kitty's dilemma and in the drama as a whole. We may remain mere spectators of the conflict between John Bell and his workers, of the intellectual debate between Chatterton and the Quaker or Chatterton and Beckford; but Kitty must be answered. It is through her that the audience participates most directly in the drama and it is this that makes her love for Chatterton more than just a sentimental embellishment.

Vigny, in a letter written from Surrey in 1836, says of London that 'vous y verriez presque dans chaque maison un gros John Bell et une blonde et triste Kitty Bell entourée d'enfants' (*6*, p.23), implying that he had painted an accurate picture of the English middle class in *Chatterton*. The modern reader may find it hard to accept Kitty's naiveté and prudery (e.g. in the scene with the Lords, pp.64-68), but a French audience in 1835 would have had less difficulty in doing so. The plausibility of the character is less important than the fact that, given her innocence and lack of self-awareness, she becomes a central source of meaning in the play. She conveys the claustrophobic atmosphere of the household, which is also that of a bourgeois society, both in her relationship with her tyrannical husband and in the constraints on her communication with Chatterton.

By analogy, she also highlights certain key features of Chatterton's character. Like him, she is a battleground on which contradictions are drawn up like opposing armies. She loves Chatterton, but resents his intrusion into her life (p.71); she wants his happiness, but fears that it will destroy his need for her (p.62); she has an intuitive understanding of him, but suspects that he may have deceived her (p.74); she wants to be near him, but is afraid that remaining in her house may prove fatal to him (p.87). These inner conflicts and her vulnerability not only create a bond between her and Chatterton, but allow them finally to be united in death, since they make plausible the play's contention that knowledge of her true feelings will kill her. Both she and Chatterton die when they realise the incompatibility of their nature with the society in which they live.

In this way, her love corresponds to the poet's dedication to his art (though the wider implication, that women in general find fulfilment in love as men do in work, which would have been taken for granted by Vigny's audience, is at most only suggested obliquely and it should be remembered that in the character of John Bell, as well as in other writings, Vigny showed himself acutely conscious of the secondary role accorded to women in a male-dominated society and their oppression by men). Just as Chatterton conceives his poetry to be a quasi-religious vocation, requiring monastic calm and dedication, so Kitty portrays her act of charity towards Chatterton as something sacred (p.55) — sanctified, we realise, by her love rather than by the Christian duty she alleges — and asserts that the Lords have broken into a solitude which she implies is like that of a nun: 'j'avais étendu sur moi la solitude comme un voile' (p.72). Her remark that she envies the Catholics their confession (pp.72-73), parallels Chatterton's that he would be a Trappist monk (p.81). There are other parallels, too, such as that between Chatterton's jealousy and her suspicion of him, after the scene with the young Lords; but I will look at this in greater detail in the next chapter.

'Après avoir bien réfléchi sur la destinée des femmes dans tous les temps et chez toutes les nations, j'ai fini par penser que tout homme devrait dire à chaque femme, au lieu de Bonjour: — Pardon! car les plus forts on fait la loi', Vigny wrote in his journal (*20*, p.107); and the same idea inspires the Quaker's speech to Rachel (coinciding with Chatterton's first appearance on stage):

> De frayeur en frayeur, tu passeras ta vie d'esclave. Peur de ton père, peur de ton mari un jour, jusqu'à la délivrance...
> — Joue, belle enfant, jusqu'à ce que tu sois femme; oublie jusque-là, et après, oublie encore si tu peux... (p.49)

Both Chatterton and Kitty are victims of a particular form of social oppression. Though it is her love for him that makes her aware of her situation, it is not the cause. Kitty has been

compared to Phèdre, in Racine's play, or to Shakespearean
heroines like Ophelia — and in the Quaker's exclamation 'Oh!
femme! faible femme!' (p.73) there may be an echo of Hamlet's
'frailty, thy name is woman'; but the identification of Kitty with
the workers whom her husband also persecutes, the depiction of
her as a victim not only of her own passions and inner conflicts,
but also of social oppression, gives her a dimension lacking from
these earlier tragic heroines. It is not just that Kitty's love creates
conflicts in her and requires a dedication from her comparable
to that which Chatterton must give to his art; rather, it is that his
dedication to poetry makes Chatterton like Kitty, forced to
recognise his slavery: the poet is thus comparable to the woman,
an outcast in a utilitarian world.

John Bell, Lord Talbot, Lord Beckford

One of the most interesting sub-themes in Vigny's play is the
identification of two forms of tyranny: that which John Bell
exercises over his family and that which he exercises over his
workers. Vigny was later to protest that he did not intend the
play to be understood as an attack on the middle class, but
whatever he intended the result is certainly a powerful critique of
the materialist and utilitarian attitudes which characterised the
bourgeoisie of his time. Both the introduction of workers on
stage and Vigny's concern with social questions were new in
French drama, though they reflected the concern of the
Romantics at the time of the 1830 Revolution with political
problems as well as the enhanced status they gave to women.
Neither of these attitudes should be confused with modern
feminism or socialism: Vigny, like Stendhal, was essentially an
aristocrat, looking back towards the pre-industrial paternalism
of the eighteenth century, though he had recently been attracted
to the utopian socialism of Saint-Simon and he may have been
aware of the writings of such pioneers of women's rights as
Mary Wollstonecraft. He was also aware of the Luddite violence
in England during the 1820s when men resisted the introduction
of new machines with sabotage because they feared that auto-
mation would take away their jobs, and he may have been

inspired by d'Haussez's book *La Grande-Bretagne en 1833* which dealt with these questions. His main objection, however, was to the class of *nouveaux riches*, the financial aristocracy who had taken power under Louis Philippe after 1830, replacing the less materialist Bourbon aristocracy. His view of the new ruling class is encapsulated in the Quaker's remark that 'la société deviendra comme ton cœur, elle aura pour dieu un lingot d'or et pour Souverain-Pontife un usurier juif' (p.47).

John Bell, 'l'homme riche, le spéculateur heureux...l'égoïste par excellence, le juste selon la loi' (p.43), therefore belongs to a new class which Vigny deliberately compares to the old aristo-cracy, while asserting its leading role in society, when he describes Bell as a monarch among his subjects (p.44). The ideology of this class is the doctrine of free trade and free enter-prise, an article of its faith that any man can achieve success through hard work and obedience to the law. The scene in which Bell confronts his workers (I, 2) summarises the attitude of these industrial barons and the social conflicts which brought them into conflict with the men they employed. John Bell's totally materialist outlook on life and his language — pompous, plati-tudinous, self-satisfied and self-assured — may have been intended to caricature the English middle class, but Vigny could hardly complain if his audience understood it as applying equally to the French bourgeoisie. His dislike of the character is shown in Bell's fawning attitude to his social superiors (in contrast to his contempt for those beneath him), and in the way in which he shows all Bell's relationships, including that with his wife, to be dominated by his materialism: he sees his wife and children as mere possessions to be exploited (p.46) and it is the argument over the accounts which links John Bell to the main plot, making his attitudes relevant to the developing love between Kitty and Chatterton.

Though Beckford is treated in a similarly unsympathetic manner, it is for rather different reasons which I shall examine in Chapter 5. Nonetheless, Vigny intends us to establish a link between the two characters because of their reduction of all values to the utilitarian philosophy which both characters share. Lord Talbot is different. His attitude to Kitty (pp.65-66) is flippant at first, but he has a genuine regard for Chatterton and when he realises that his friend is upset, he tells the other Lords not to overdo their banter (p.67). In Act III, scene 4, we see him in a new light, sincerely concerned about Chatterton's prospects and anxious to do all he can to help. 'Je suis surpris que vous n'ayez pas compté sur moi plutôt' (p.94), he tells Chatterton whom he defends against Beckford by insisting that he is a friend (p.97). So, despite his insensitivity and his cavalier attitude in the earlier part of the play, he emerges by the end as a loyal and generous figure, though powerless to help. If he stands for anything, it is the qualities of the old aristocracy, insouciant, pleasure-loving, but appreciative of the arts and ready to patronise them and, at the very least, committed to values other than the purely materialist ones which John Bell represents. Hard-drinking (p.66), hard-riding (p.67), unintellectual (p.64), he is certainly no *martyr*, but he is not entirely to be identified with the *bourreaux*. In the scene with Beckford he is even allowed to take over in part the role played in *Stello*, in the corresponding scene, by Le Docteur Noir, while his occasional archaic turn of speech suggests that his type is becoming an anachronism in a world increasingly devoted to the making of money: 'Il n'y faut pas songer' (p.90), for example, where the position of the pronoun belongs to eighteenth-century rather than to modern French.

Vigny's skill as a dramatist is shown particularly in the way in which he adapts the language to the character and it is this point that I have tried to bring out in this chapter and that I would like to emphasise here. Even the minor characters of Talbot, Beckford and Bell speak in language which allows us to identify them immediately and it is this, rather than any description in Vigny's preliminary notes or the comments of the Quaker, that fixes the characters for us. He shows equal skill in the construction of the play, using a number of devices to hold our attention and carry the action along. But without characters in whom we can believe, these devices would create only an empty shell and the ideas that Vigny tries to express might as well have been advanced in an essay as in a dramatic work. The characters, and the text they speak, are the play: the rest is merely what we choose to insert above the lines or in the silences between them.

4. 'L'action matérielle'

S'il existait une intrigue moins compliquée que celle-ci, je
la choisirais. L'action matérielle est assez peu de chose
pourtant...C'est l'histoire d'un homme qui a écrit une
lettre le matin, et qui attend la réponse jusqu'au soir; elle
arrive, et le tue. (pp.33-34)

Though hardly adequate as a description of the play, this
summary of the plot of *Chatterton* stresses two important
points; the first, obviously, is Vigny's deliberate striving towards
simplicity with the aim of concentrating attention on the ideas
which animate this *drame de la pensée*; the second, more
paradoxically in a work devoted to the representation of
abstractions, is the part played by physical objects such as the
Lord Mayor's letter, because it is to a large extent around them
that the dramatist structures his work and through them that he
reveals the character and attitudes of the people involved.

There are comparisons and contrasts to be made here with the
dramatic method of Shakespeare, as it was understood in
Vigny's time. It is no accident that the most powerful expression
of French Romantic theory, Stendhal's *Racine et Shakespeare*,
should have chosen to personify two contrasting approaches to
literature by setting against the purest exponent of Classical
drama, the English playwright who could still be referred to by
critics in the 1820s as a drunken savage and, more moderately,
dismissed as a genius whose misfortune was to have lived in an
age devoid of any understanding of the aesthetic demands and
principles of drama. What these critics dismissed as
Shakespeare's defects, Stendhal and Hugo had claimed as his
strengths and offered as a model for the new Romantic drama:
the disregard of the three unities of time, place and action and
the mixture of comedy and tragedy most clearly exhibited in Act
II, scene 3 of *Macbeth* where, immediately following the murder

of Duncan, the Porter enters with a stream of comic and bawdy abuse, lowering the tension, but at the same time heightening by contrast the horror of what has gone before.

In 1834, Alfred de Musset published *Lorenzaccio*, the most perfectly 'Shakespearean' of French Romantic dramas (and indeed requiring so many characters and changes of scene that Musset published it in a series called *Un Spectacle dans un fauteuil* and it was considered impossible to stage until the end of the century). Hugo's dramas had also deliberately ignored the unities and Vigny, as translator of *Othello* and *The Merchant of Venice*, had before him examples of plays with sub-plots, where the action is extended over several months and takes place in different settings. But in *Chatterton* he has deliberately tried to ignore these possibilities, confining himself to the events of a single day and setting them (except for the first two scenes at the beginning of Act III) entirely in the living room of John Bell's house. The one change of scene, to Chatterton's bedroom, would have been impossible to avoid without artificiality, though Vigny originally hoped to minimise it by combining the two locations into one set, having to abandon this for the actual production because of difficulties in staging.

Whether he respects the rule of unity of action is another matter. The whole second act of the play has been criticised as a sentimental irrelevance and the scene between John Bell and his workers might be said to have little bearing on Chatterton's personal tragedy. If, as Vigny made out in the slightly whimsical summary quoted earlier, *Chatterton* is no more than the story of the poet's unsuccessful attempt to solicit the patronage of the Lord Mayor, then the other characters and the scenes in which they appear are all open to the charge of irrelevance. Of course, there is more to it than that and both Kitty's love and John Bell's materialism are directly relevant to the question of the nature of poetic genius and society's attitudes to it. Even though the underlying themes of the play and the integration of all its elements may not be evident while it is unfolding to a spectator in the theatre, he is bound to be impressed by the concentration of the action. Even the Lords, whose clowning might have provided the occasion for comic relief, are not allowed to

develop as humorous characters but kept in check by the
audience's immediate awareness of the pain they inflict on Kitty
and Chatterton. There is no lightening of the tone, no real sub-
plot, no element of melodrama that is not explicity related to the
situation of the two central characters.

The language of the play is also remarkable for its restraint.
Vigny has chosen to write in prose (as recommended by
Stendhal, but perhaps unexpected for a poet, writing about
poetry and faced with the examples of Shakespeare, Racine and
Hugo); and it is a prose notable for its avoidance of 'poetic'
effects, using a relatively limited vocabulary and short on the
descriptive adjectives which would add colour and emphasis.
Even Chatterton's longer monologue (pp.79-82), the clearest
piece of rhetoric in the play, with its succession of exclamations
('Oh! dégradation! oh! honteux travail!', etc.) and its abrupt
shifts of course ('...je ne lui répondrai pas! Si! par le Ciel! je lui
répondrai!'), contains few genuinely descriptive epithets and
those that it does use are not thrown in merely for effect: they
underlie the entire passage, showing, despite the apparently
random wandering of the speaker's thought, the real pain that
he suffers. There are those which express the idea of physical
collapse: *malade, mutilé, stérile, délabrée*; or poverty and want:
pauvre (three times), *misérable* (twice), *froid* (twice), *glacé,
malheureux, rude, profane, honteux, vile*; or emptiness: *blanc*
(twice, with this significance), *pâle*. In contrast, are those which
recall the qualities of Chatterton's character which may allow
him to resist this *humiliation toute nouvelle: cette fierté
naturelle, cet esprit rebelle, esprit superbe, Paria intelligent*.
Finally, (and this covers practically all the epithet adjectives used
in the passage), there are the terms he uses in evoking his father,
in positive contrast to this picture of himself: *bon vieux marin,
franc capitaine, beau front* and *cheveux blancs*. The adjectives
used as attributes of the verb reinforce the same overall
impression: note, for example, the contrast in *mes mains sont
glacées, ma tête est brûlante*, introducing the theme of physical
deprivation and mental agitation; the repetition of the phrase *il
est certain* at the two points where he reveals his preoccupation
with Kitty's love; and the linked exclamations *je suis perdu! oui,*

perdu! and *ne suis-je donc pas libre? plus libre que jamais?*, the first, showing his realisation of an impossible situation, leading to the second as he weighs up its implications.

The language of the play, in the same way as the language of Racine, hides its complexities behind an unornamented surface and achieves its effects not by verbal ingenuity or invention, but by repetition and reinforcement. I have already mentioned the importance, in the speech of the Quaker, of certain key words and the way in which they are used as leitmotifs throughout the play: *cœur, âme, esprit, sauvage, primitif*, conveying the qualities peculiar to the *martyrs*, qualities of feeling and sensitivity which distinguish them from the *bourreaux* and explain the hostility of society towards them. In the same way, the *bourreaux* are defined by words like *calcul, chiffre* and, above all, *utile*. Expressions referring to sickness and fever prepare for Chatterton's ironical 'Je suis guéri. — Seulement j'ai la tête brûlante' (p.102); and *l'obstiné Suicide* (p.76) is evoked, before the Quaker's direct reference to it, and subsequently, by paraphrase and allusion, so that the word hovers constantly at the back of the spectator's (or reader's) mind. *Ami, riche/pauvre, grâce, miséricorde, faible/fort, fatal*, other references to religion and destiny, *poésie* (of course), *rêve, imagination* — each acquires a peculiar resonance within the context of the work.

This purity of language, together with the near obedience to the unities, suggest a development from Racinian tragedy rather than a revolt against it and I have already mentioned the comparison drawn between Kitty and a Racinian figure like Phèdre. In certain other respects, too, *Chatterton* shows similarities with the techniques of Classical tragedy, in the way in which we are introduced to the characters in the first scene, for example, and the role of the Quaker as the confidant of the two lovers, which recalls a stock figure from seventeenth-century drama. Vigny may have been influenced unconsciously as much as consciously by his knowledge of the Classical theatre and his ambition, to make this a philosophical play, demands that he should reject some of the cloak-and-dagger melodrama which Hugo so greatly enjoyed.

However, this is not merely a Classical tragedy in disguise.

The very idea of a *drame de la pensée*, as Vigny was aware, was new in the French theatre and many of the means he employs would not have been acceptable in Classical drama. Though in fact the ban on violent action on stage was less absolute in Racine's day than is sometimes suggested, Chatterton's drinking of the poison and Kitty's death in full view of the audience would not have been acceptable and are clearly 'Shakespearean', as are the influence of *Hamlet* in Chatterton's two monologues, in his general character as a man in whom 'la rêverie continuelle a tué l'action' (p.51) and the theme of suicide; and the use of objects such as the Bible, the letter and the phial of opium as a focus for the action and a means of linking the scenes. The concern for local colour is also a Romantic element: the Quaker, the references to John Bell's factory at 'Norton', to duelling on Primrose Hill (p.66), to tea (p.66), to Garrick (p.64), to London fog (p.81), etc. This concern to situate the drama in a particular time and place would have been alien to Classical tragedy: the spirit of *Chatterton* like the feelings, the ideas and the attitudes expressed by its characters, belongs to the nineteenth century.

The use of objects in developing the plot and exposing the feelings of the protagonists is something that Vigny almost certainly learned from *Othello* where Desdemona's hand-kerchief serves as a key element in the progress of Othello's jealousy. The same object which for Othello is a token of his love and its loss definite proof of his wife's infidelity, is for her a comparatively trivial thing; she knows that she is not responsible for its loss and has no idea of her husband's suspicions, so she lies, assuming that it will soon be found and not realising that her lack of concern will be seen by her husband as further evidence of her corrupt nature. The incident in *Chatterton* when John Bell confronts Kitty with the accounts which reveal that she has lent money to Chatterton to pay his debts (pp.47-48, 55-57), though less crucial to the plot, helps to inform us of Kitty's feeling for Chatterton, while her own conviction of her innocence, in contrast to John's growing jealousy (to emerge later in Act III, scene 4), are strongly reminiscent of *Othello*.

The accounts are referred to at various points in the play, reinforcing the evidence which they provide of Kitty's feeling for

her lodger; so, too, does the Bible, a silent token of their love,
surfacing in the three acts (Act I, scene 1, Act II, scene 1 and Act
III, scene 3). Like Kitty's rhetorical questions, they leave the
audience to fill in their significance, helping to establish the
drama beneath the surface of the play, the 'intertext' (to use a
fashionable piece of jargon) which the reader has to spell out for
himself. The significance of the phial of opium is made rather
more explicit, but it is comparable in its repeated appearances.
The letter, which Chatterton mentions on his first appearance
(p.50), has the most evident relevance to the development of the
plot and leads directly to the scene with Lord Beckford which is
a hinge for the action and for the exposition of the guiding
theme.

It is not only objects that are used in this way. As I said at the
start of Chapter 3, Vigny has paid close attention to the dress of
his characters to create contrast and atmosphere. Throughout
the play, while our attention may be concentrated on the
martyrs, we are reminded of the presence of the *bourreaux*
behind the scenes: by John Bell's voice off-stage in Act I, scene 1
(p.41, 43), by the shouts and cracking of whips from the hunting
party (p.62), by the sound of the Lord Mayor's coach (p.94). In
the same way, during Chatterton's monologue (p.79, 81), the
sound of the clock striking not only marks the passage of time,
but tolls a knell like that which tells Faustus that his time is
nearly up.

If we now go back to consider the total structure of the play,
we can see that these physical elements outside the text fit into a
pattern of development and structure. The first act, as well as
introducing the characters and demonstrating the importance of
Chatterton by preparing his entry in scene 4 (p.49), sets up all
the elements which will eventually lead to the play's tragic outcome. We are informed of the lack of sympathy and communication within John Bell's household, asked to compare John
Bell's treatment of his workers with that of his family and led to
appreciate Kitty's unhappiness, which links her with Chatterton:
his first appearance allows the Quaker to make the link explicit
in his remark about *martyrs et bourreaux* ('Tu seras toujours
martyr de tous, comme la mère de cette enfant-là', p.50). He

also comments ironically on his weariness with life, mentions the letter and, in his subsequent conversation with the Quaker, introduces some of the themes that will emerge from his conversation with Beckford and his monologue: the need for the poet to have time for reflection, the value of his contribution to the national life, the inevitability of his vocation. The act ends with the scene between Kitty and John Bell, gradually revealing its real significance as we realise that the matter of the accounts has to do more with Kitty's feeling for Chatterton than the aridity of her relationship with her husband.

Act II opens on the mystery of Chatterton's desire for concealment, leading to the misunderstanding between the two lovers, the scene with the Lords and the resulting jealousy which Chatterton experiences, corresponding to Kitty's feeling that she has been deceived in him. While the lack of direct communication between the two characters and their subsequent misunderstanding may appear to parallel the failure of communication in Kitty's relationship with John Bell, in fact they reveal precisely the opposite: the reticence of the two lovers, because of their strength of feeling, and their gradual awareness of their love. But by the end of the act, Kitty is made aware too of the barriers to any development of the relationship and the still more threatening danger from Chatterton's obsession with suicide. The sentimental interest of this second act may seem irrelevant to the central theme of the play, but in fact it is not. Kitty's love illustrates the sympathy and understanding that might, in other circumstances, create a climate in which Chatterton could develop his genius, while her persecution by the same repressive social forces that drive him to his death, establishes a continuity in the utilitarian outlook of a class which subject poets and women to judgement by the same criteria of economics and power.

Act III, opening with Chatterton's apparently disordered monologue, brings together all the motifs of the previous two acts. Its events are designed to delay an outcome which we know is inevitable; the Quaker's plea to Chatterton, the visit of Lord Beckford, the admission of love. Beckford's visit, combined with Chatterton's awareness of Kitty's feelings for him and the sympathetic attitude of Talbot, seems to have averted the crisis, but it is followed by the double *coup de théâtre* of Chatterton's discovery of the attacks on his name and the reading of the letter in which Beckford offers him a place as valet. Neither love nor the efforts of individuals can triumph over a social system which accords no status to living poets. Chatterton accomplishes his martyrdom and Kitty, whose weak heart has already been mentioned, follows him. The play itself and the respect we give to Chatterton's name are evidence of society's exploitation, after his death, of the genius of the 'marvellous boy who perished in his pride'. Ironically, it is this apotheosis, not his work, that allows Vigny to elevate him to the symbolic status of The Poet, detaching the qualities of the man from the quality of what he made.

5. 'Un drame de la pensée'

'La maladie est incurable', remarks the Quaker and, when Chatterton asks: 'La mienne?', repies:

> Non, celle de l'humanité. — Selon ton cœur, tu prends en bienveillante pitié ceux qui te disent: Sois un autre homme que celui que tu es; — moi, selon ma tête, je les ai en mépris, parce qu'ils veulent dire: Retire-toi de notre soleil; il n'y a pas de place pour toi. (p.54)

But Chatterton, throughout his answer, carries on speaking quietly to Rachel: it is not the place of the mythical hero to understand his own role in the myth.

The Quaker's reply not only points to the social dimension of the drama, but shows also that its target is specifically the ruling class in society, those whose enjoyment of the sunshine incites them to exclude any individual subject to other laws than the ones they have devised for their own benefit and the main-tenance of their power. Literally, the class under attack must be the industrial bourgeoisie and the aristocracy of wealth in Britain in the 1770s, represented by John Bell and Lord Beckford; but the scene between Bell and his workmen shows that Vigny was in touch with such events as the Luddite violence of the 1820s in Britain, while the development of industrial-isation and the establishment after the Revolution of July 1830 in France of a régime modelled to some extent on the lines of British parliamentary democracy, convinced many of his contemporaries that his real target was the French bourgeoisie and the class, defined at the time as *l'aristocratie d'argent*, which was rapidly acknowledged to have been the main beneficiary of the change of power.

Vigny himself protested that his play should not be taken as an attack on the middle class, and what I want to demonstrate in this chapter are the sources of some of the ideas in a work which is considerably more subtle than merely a political pamphlet under the guise of a defence of poetry. What Vigny confronts in *Chatterton* is not just a materialist class but an ideology, that of the Liberal bourgeoisie of the 1820s; he confronts it, but at the same time finds himself obliged to argue his case on terms which are largely those laid down by his opponents. He is not alone in this, since the Romantic debate on literature in general, and poetry in particular, took place in the context of a view of history and culture that was formed during the eighteenth century and, though challenged from the early years of the nineteenth century, retained a considerable hold in the minds even of those who appeared to reject its conclusions.

The Romantic movement in literature and art is generally presented in grossly simplified terms, like a football match in which the new side of Romanticism is pitted against the old guard of Classicists, with their adherence to the outworn dogmas of Racinian tragedy. Of course, the contest was not simply one of Racine vs. Shakespeare and the very wide spectrum of ideas represented by the leading Romantic writers, as well as the changes in their attitudes even during the relatively short period of the decade 1820-1830 (when Hugo, for example, evolved from a reactionary right-wing political stance to a left-wing one), should make us doubt any simplified view of the debate. Moreover, the study of the literary and political press of the period will show that opposition to Romanticism did not by any means come solely from critics who would have liked to see a return to the literature of the seventeenth and eighteenth centuries. There was a body of opposition to the new movement, which may be broadly described as 'Liberal', basing its hostility to Romanticism on a broad ideology of human culture; this Liberal group was in fact highly influential in French intellectual life and its politics attracted, or came to attract, many of the young writers now associated with the Romantic movement.

For various reasons, it had become a cliché by the early 1830s that poetry was dead and that the more extravagant manifestations of Romanticism were symptoms connected with the exhaustion of the poetic impulse. Hugo, in his preface to *Marion de Lorme* acknowledges the existence of this view when he says that 'il y a des esprits, et dans le nombre fort élevé, qui disent que la poésie est morte' — though, as a poet, he naturally goes on to refute the idea. By 1831, when he was writing, even this gambit of putting up the statement in order to refute it had become something of a cliché.

Since the decade of the 1820s had seen the publication of large numbers of volumes of poetry, and a vital new movement represented by such poets as Hugo and Lamartine, the conviction that the poetic spirit was either dead or dying could only come from a particular concept of what constituted 'poetry' allied to a system of ideas that supported the view that poetry was in some way unsuited to the climate of the modern age. This view rested on two main arguments: firstly that civilisations developed along a pattern comparable to that of individual human development, from infancy to childhood, maturity and old age; and secondly, that the forms by which cultures expressed themselves also varied, certain types of poetry being more appropriate to early development, others to later stages, and other literary genres taking over as mankind progressed. I have stated this general idea in highly schematic terms, but the metaphors that derived from it and were used to express it, were in fact quite convincing and a good deal more pervasive than one might at first glance suppose. Indeed, it is not difficult to find examples even today of writers who hold to some points of this view: for example, that lyric poetry is peculiar to the work of young poets, that epic poetry is associated especially with the early stages of cultural development or that certain forms of poetry are 'outmoded' or impossible to produce in a contemporary context.

Hugo, in his preface to *Cromwell*, casually introduced the historical section of his argument in the following terms:

Le genre humain dans son ensemble a grandi, s'est développé, a mûri comme un de nous. Il a été enfant, il a été homme, nous assistons maintenant à son imposante vieillesse. (*15*, p.20)

And, like most others who use the analogy, Hugo naturally sees his own time as corresponding to one of the more advanced stages of development (though some prefer to speak of 'maturity' rather than 'old age', however imposing!).

Death is what follows old age, so this analogy with human life had depressing connotations which appeared to be in direct conflict with the idea of progress and the perfectibility of man. The Liberal of the 1820s was generally optimistic about the outlook for human society and would not have accepted willingly that mankind was entering its dotage. A way out of the problem had been provided by one of the most widely-studied literary theorists of the time. Madame de Staël, in her book *De la littérature considérée dans ses rapports avec les institutions sociales* (1800), saw the doctrine of perfectibility as applying in different ways to science and art. In the case of the latter, a point was reached beyond which literature and the fine arts could not hope to progress, while science was capable of unending advance. Not that art would be condemned necessarily to decadence, but its further development would be dependent on that of the moral, philosophical and natural sciences:

> Lorsque la littérature d'imagination a atteint dans une langue le plus haut degré de perfection dont elle est susceptible, il faut que le siècle suivant appartienne à la philosophie, pour que l'esprit humain ne cesse pas de faire des progrès. (*24*, pp.173-74).

This leads her to the statement that 'la poésie d'imagination ne fera plus de progrès en France' (*24*, p.359).

Though the essential word here is *progrès* — Madame de Staël was not saying that there was no place at all for poetry in advanced societies — her arguments were borrowed to support the theory that poetry was a dying art and her qualification (*la poésie d'imagination*) developed as the basis of a fairly precise definition of poetry itself:

> La poésie est éminemment allégorique...son attribut essentiel consiste dans la faculté d'individualiser, c'est-à-

dire de personnifier les sentiments et les passions de
l'homme...' (*8*, pp.310-11)

What is interesting about this is that the much-admired critic
Schlegel had written of Greek poetry that its main characteristic
was that it 'donne de l'âme aux sentiments et un corps aux
pensées' (*21*, p.30); and Ballanche, a few lines later in the
passage quoted above, concludes: 'Ainsi la poésie des anciens est
la seule vraie poésie'. Moreover Schlegel's succinct definition of
the allegorical character of Greek poetry was taken up by Victor
Chauvet, who wrote that ancient Greece possessed:

> ...un climat délicieux, un sol couvert de fleurs, une religion
> remplissant au plus haut degré la condition de toute poésie,
> de prêter une âme à la matière et un corps à la pensée.
> (*Revue encyclopédique*, XXVII, 1825, pp.323-24)

And yet again by Michelet when he speaks of the characteristic
of the Ancients being their ability to 'prêter la vie aux êtres
inanimés, prêter un corps aux choses immatérielles' (*26*, p.xx).

The Greeks, then, in the 'infancy' of mankind, had enjoyed a
peculiar aptitude for lyric poetry, and the nineteenth-century
writers I have quoted were only in this following the eighteenth-
century critic Denina who firmly asserted that lyric poetry in the
age of Pindar had attained 'un point de majesté et d'élévation
inaccessible à tout autre (âge)' (*14*, p.19), even though, as he
went on to admit, hardly any examples of all this poetry have
survived! As an anonymous writer in the *Revue encyclopédique*
remarked, summing up all the elements of this particular
argument:

> Il en est de la poésie pour les peuples comme des illusions
> de la jeunesse pour les individus: on a beau les regretter;
> vouloir rester sous leur empire, ce serait renoncer à l'âge
> mûr... L'idée du beau présidait à la civilisation antique;
> celle du vrai, du juste et de l'utile domine de plus en plus
> dans la société moderne. Si ses croyances étaient restées
> poétiques, elles ne seraient plus en harmonie avec sa
> raison. (XXXIX, 1828, p.117)

The word *utile* brings us back to the context of *Chatterton* after what may at first sight appear to have been a long and irrelevant digression. But these ideas on poetry, which constituted the critical orthodoxy at the time when Vigny was writing and during the period when his thought was developing, are anything but irrelevant to a play which sets out to defend poets and poetry against the charge that they serve no useful purpose in the modern world. The quotations that I have given are necessarily only a small selection, but the interest of even the theme of Ancient Greece appears immediately if one turns, not to *Chatterton* itself, but to *Stello* and to the scene of the discussion with Lord Beckford which Vigny shortened when transferring it to the stage:

> Imagination! dit M. Beckford, toujours l'imagination au lieu du bon sens et du jugement! Pour être Poète à la façon lyrique et somnambule dont vous l'êtes, il faudrait vivre sous le ciel de Grèce, marcher avec des sandales, une chlamyde et les jambes nues, et faire danser les pierres avec la psaltérion. (pp.137-38)

There is no obvious reason why Beckford, seeking an image to fix his idea of the perfect conditions for lyric poetry, and addressing his remarks to a poet whose imaginative world revolved around medieval Europe, should have envisaged him in Greek dress playing a psaltery; except that in Vigny's mind this vision of the ideal conditions for lyric poetry was associated with attacks from those who, like Beckford, judged poetry to be out of place in a modern age ruled by doctrines of utility.

Of course, with the evidence of the volumes of verse which flowed from the publishers year by year, not all writers on the subject imagined that the 'maturity' of society would simply kill off poetry. Beckford himself admits to having written verses in his youth but emphasises that 'un bon Anglais doit être utile au pays' (p.96). He would have agreed with Madame de Staël when she said:

> Heureux le pays où les écrivains sont tristes, où les
> commerçants sont satisfaits, les riches mélancoliques et les
> hommes du peuple contents!. (*24*, p.227)

(except, of course, for her condemnation of the rich). The view
that social and political progress is bound to lead to the alienation from society of such exceptional individuals as poets and
artists, was that of an anonymous writer in the *Revue encyclopédique* who saw in the United States of America a model for
the society of the future:

> Ce peuple nous offre une image prophétique des temps
> vers lesquels s'achemine la civilisation du monde chrétien,
> temps prospère pour la science, pour la morale et pour la
> liberté publique, temps doux et calmes pour le gros du
> genre humain, ...mais stériles et douloureux pour ces âmes
> particulières que la nature, se trompant d'époque, aura
> douées des besoins du génie poétique. (XLV, 1830, p.33)

Who better than Chatterton, tormented by 'la passion de la
pensée' (p.52), taking on the habit of the medieval monk
Rowley, to represent a man born out of his time? It was a feeling
well understood by Vigny, aristocrat and stoic, who shared with
Chatterton his loathing of modern commercial civilisation.

Oddly enough, however, if there was one country which
seemed to disprove the idea that industrial civilisation was
unlikely to encourage the production of poetry, it was England.
As L. Simond had remarked in his account of a journey to
England in 1810 and 1811,

> L'enfance de la civilisation est l'âge poétique des nations,
> et voici pourtant un vieux peuple, riche et commerçant,
> froid et calculateur, plus fertile en véritables poètes depuis
> dix ans qu'il ne l'a jamais été... (*23*, pp.454-55)

But this neither contradicted the image of a society founded on
the materialist values of money and devoted to cold science, nor
did it guarantee that the poets born into such a society would

achieve happiness or acceptance in it. What Vigny and other poets of his time would retain in these comments, was a definition of society and socially useful work that excluded imaginative literature and seemed to force them, with almost a scientific inevitability, into the role of social outcasts.

There were, however, some doctrines which appeared for a time to offer an alternative road. The most important of these, because of its influence on Vigny and some of the other Romantics, was Saint-Simonism, both the doctrines of Saint-Simon and the later development of these doctrines after his death in 1825.

The basis of Saint-Simon's 'New Christian' social order was its reliance on leadership by a sort of troika composed of industrialists, scientists and artists. The artists' mission was an almost priestly one, of guiding mankind towards the future (though, as was pointed out at the time, some Saint-Simonists were inclined to give artists the more prosaic role of propagandists for the new order and, had they ever gained power, would probably have been ruthlessly hostile to those who did not share and proclaim their views). What is interesting about Saint-Simonism, in the context of *Chatterton*, is that it conceded the point that artists must be found some *useful* role in modern society, instead of adopting, for example, a concept of 'art for art's sake', or a view of artists as guardians of culture, or entertainers, or those who expressed the higher aspirations of mankind, or some other non-materialist interpretation of their function. As Marguerite Thibert says:

> ...l'évolution générale du saint-simonisme entraînait la théorie sociale de l'art qu'on y professait vers un mysticisme esthétique curieusement mitigé d'utilitarisme. (*25*, p.25)

So, when Chatterton offers his answer to Lord Beckford, it is to show the poet as the one who 'lit dans les astres la route que nous montre le doigt du Seigneur' and to emphasise that 'nous sommes tous de l'équipage, et nul n'est inutile dans la manœuvre de notre glorieux navire' (p.97), framing his defence in utilitarian terms which will not only be understood by Beckford, but which are those laid down by the Lord Mayor and his like as the only terms on which the argument can be conducted. It is significant that Vigny's image of the poet as navigator was subsequently borrowed in Saint-Simonian poetry.

By the time he came to write *Chatterton*, however, Vigny had become disillusioned with Saint-Simonism, and the reflection of his brief flirtation with Saint-Simonian doctrines comes rather from the episode in *Stello* (when he was still to some extent attracted by them), than from his convictions at the time of writing the play. Even by the last episode of *Stello* (that dealing with André Chénier), he was evidently disaffected from the idea of the new social order and had come to hold the view that all régimes were necessarily hostile to poets.

The image of the poet as the one who searches the stars for the road that society should take is strikingly similar to that offered by Shelley in his *Defence of Poetry*:

> Poets are the hierophants of an unapprehended inspiration; the mirrors of the gigantic shadows which futurity casts upon the present... Poets are the unacknowledged legislators of the world. (*22*, p.159)

I am not the first to compare this with Chatterton's speech, but I am perhaps the first to point out that Shelley's defence was written in answer to precisely the same view of human history and civilisation that I have been discussing in this chapter. In his essay *The Four Ages of Poetry*, Shelley's friend Thomas Love Peacock had argued that human civilisation progresses through different stages and that the modern age, with its scientific and utilitarian preoccupations, is necessarily hostile to works of the imagination. In response, Shelley argued the universal validity of poetry, its leading role in society and its moral significance, even when those who produce it are themselves not outstanding for their moral qualities:

> But even whilst they deny and abjure, they are yet compelled to serve, the power which is seated on the throne of their own soul. (*22*, p.159)

Vigny could not have known Shelley's work which, though written in 1821, was not published until 1840. The similarity in their concepts of the poet and his role in society (though I would not want to suggest that it is especially profound), can only come from their sensitivity to the climate of their times. In Vigny's case, he chose to depict the oppressive tendency of this society in two ways: indirectly through the person of John Bell, a philistine tyrant who persecutes his workmen and his wife; and directly, as far as poets are concerned, in Lord Beckford, a cultured and powerful man who is nonetheless fatally unequipped to appreciate Chatterton's sensitivity or his genius. What Beckford represents (most evidently in *Stello* where his opinions are developed at greater length than in the play), is not an English gentleman of the eighteenth century so much as a liberal bourgeois of Vigny's own time and country.

If Vigny seems largely to accept, at the end of *Stello*, that all political régimes will, for different reasons, prove hostile to poets, in *Chatterton* he has taken his thesis onto the public stage and made it rather more clearly a plea for positive action. It is a theme on which he expands in the 'Dernière nuit de travail', while fully aware of the problems he has raised. The idea of the poet which he puts forward is élitist — the contrary, for example, of the supposition underlying a modern 'poetry workshop' or the publication of anthologies of poems by schoolchildren, that anyone can write poetry. For Vigny, poets are rare and it is axiomatic that the majority will not appreciate them: 'son langage choisi n'est compris que d'un petit nombre d'hommes choisi lui-même' (p.29). After a poet's death, perhaps, his genius will be recognised but in his lifetime he can expect only jealousy or indifference. The state, too, 'ne protège que les intérêts positifs' (p.29). But society *can* afford to maintain men of genius, it has the means to keep them from starvation or humiliating and soul-destroying work if it chooses to make laws for their protection:

C'est au législateur à guérir cette plaie, l'une des plus vives et des plus profondes de notre corps social; c'est à lui qu'il appartient de réaliser dans le présent une partie des jugements meilleurs de l'avenir, en assurant quelques années d'existence seulement à tout homme qui aurait donné un seul gage du talent divin. (p.33)

But the problem of identification remains, as Vigny is well aware (p.32).

A great deal of this discussion hinges on a particular concept of the poet, which includes in its turn a particular concept of poetry and in this idea, which has been implicit in much of our discussion of Chatterton as a character in the play, as well as in the subjects I have raised in this chapter, lies the central significance of the work. I said earlier that both Vigny and Shelley, in formulating their defence of poetry, did so largely on terms dictated by their opponents, by those who believed that poetry was quite simply incompatible with modern scientific society, in Vigny's own words, 'une société matérialiste, où le calculateur avare exploite sans pitié l'intelligence et le travail' (p.34); a society that was also in the throes of industrialisation, taking men and women from the rural existence which had continued largely unchanged in Europe since the Middle Ages and crowding them into towns where their labour was exploited ruthlessly by the new feudal barons like John Bell: in view of this, and given Vigny's awareness of it, one might question, as men were increasingly to do as the century wore on, whether the suffering of poets (by Vigny's own definition, a minute social minority) was indeed one of the deepest wounds in society or the one that stood in greatest need of treatment.

That apart, the reason why Vigny, like Shelley, could hardly avoid accepting some of the premises on which this opposition to poetry was based, was partly that they were both intellectuals, well-read and alive to the climate of their age; and partly that the literature of the eighteenth century in both France and Britain had been predominantly hostile to what they defined as poetry. Looking back over the previous century, Vigny could hardly do otherwise than agree that its preoccupation had been with the literature of ideas rather than with that of the imagination. Another, perhaps unexpected, point of comparison between Vigny and Shelley is that they both had considerable respect for 'philosophy' (the term they would have used to describe the genre which had produced the most characteristic works of the eighteenth century): Shelley once remarked that his highest aspiration was to be a philosopher, while Vigny's poetry is outstanding for its concentration on ideas, and *Chatterton*, which he offers as a *drame de la pensée* and an example of a genre which he believes is bound eventually to find favour with the public, is a deliberate reaction against the verse dramas of Hugo. At the heart of the play, there is this contradiction of a work which sets out to define a certain idea of The Poet and to defend him against a hostile society, but does so in prose, in an intellectual framework remarkably similar to the one which it has described as being hostile to the poetic sensibility. The conflict between head and heart, the enthusiasm of Stello and the scepticism of Le Docteur Noir, the poetry of Chatterton and the philosophy of the Quaker, was one that Vigny experienced in himself and was never to resolve.

It is a conflict that belongs peculiarly to the age of Romanticism. The eighteenth century had been well aware of the demands of both reason and sensibility and had never doubted which, in a well-ordered society, should take precedence. But by the end of the century men had begun to doubt whether society was well-ordered and to question its right to subject the individual to its demands. When, in the political sphere, a man like Napoleon Bonaparte could impose his will on half of Europe, it appeared that there were individuals who stood so far above the crowd that their nature would not permit them to recognise normal or reasonable limitations; and if, in the political sphere, such individuals were not an unmixed blessing for humanity, who could deny that they had had their counterparts in literature and the arts and that we had benefitted from the genius of Shakespeare, Leonardo or Raphael? In 'La Dernière nuit de travail', it is the Poet as a man of genius that Vigny distinguishes from the man of letters or the great writer; and if he demands for him a consideration which society can justifiably withhold from the other two, it is because he believes in the Romantic concept of genius as a gift with privileges consistent with its rarity and ultimately so precious to society that it escapes from the usual norms. If men were able to recognise the ultimate value of genius, they would be susceptible to the argument of its immediate utility.

The problem, however, in Vigny's play is that, while asserting the beneficial long-term effects of poetic genius, he has no immediate definition of it to support this view. In fact, his definition excludes the idea of utility. The Poet is not described as a producer of poetry, but as the possessor of a poetic sensibility. As we pass from the man of letters (pp.26-27), to the great writer (pp.27-28) and finally to the poet (pp.28-29), we move from the concrete production of literary works, to philosophical thought (expressed however in actual writings) and, finally, to a pure sensibility where only the phrase 'la divine forme des vers' (p.29) even hints that its vessel might deign to overflow and communicate with the world outside. The comparison of these three portraits in 'La Dernière nuit de travail', when one looks at the actual language in which they are written and notes the transition from the tangible to the intangible, is quite remarkable. The productive writer is treated with moral contempt as insincere ('dépourvu d'émotions réelles', p.26) and superficial; the great writer is defined by his relative lack of productive facility ('il marche le pas qu'il veut, sait jeter des semences à une grande profondeur, et attendre qu'elles aient germé, dans une immobilité effrayante', pp.27-28), but is in touch with the society of his time; the poet is not a writer at all, but 'une nature', described almost entirely in metaphorical terms: the emphasis is entirely on his need to *do* nothing, on the idea that any activity other than complete subjection to the needs of his sensibility will destroy his gift (p.30). The figure of Chatterton in the play is consistent with this view of the poet as one validated only by his inner conviction, his emotions and his imagination. It is no accident that Cocteau's *Les Enfants terribles*, the twentieth-century work which (as I shall show in the next chapter) owes most to *Chatterton*, is a myth of the poetic sensibility whose protagonists *live* their poetry entirely, never attempting to express it in the form of language.

The high status which Vigny accords to the poetic sensibility and the idea that poetry can be divorced not only from verse, but even from language, to become an almost abstract quality, is what more than anything makes *Chatterton* a work of its time. If I have stressed it particularly, it is because this concept of poetry, this definition of what is 'poetic', what the poet is (as opposed to what he does), still profoundly influences our own conception of poetry. Later in the nineteenth century, argu- ments of the kind used by Shelley and Vigny about the 'utility' of poetry were to be abandoned and their place taken by the doctrines of 'art for art's sake'. Even Vigny puts little conviction into the crowning image of poets as those who steer society towards the future, making it seem more like a witty demolition of Lord Beckford ('Qu'en dites-vous, mylord? lui donnez-vous tort? Le pilote n'est pas inutile', p.97), rather than a serious attempt to define the social role of the artist. In the last resort, the play is a defence of the poet as the supreme individualist, escaping utilitarian definition, the last refuge of spiritual values in a society that has abandoned religion in favour of materialism and replaced its old aristocracy with an aristocracy of wealth. Against the triumph of values he cannot share, Vigny pleads on behalf of the individual and speaks as much for the mute aspirations of Kitty Bell as in justification of the poet she loves.

6. *'Cette porte est ouverte à présent...'*

At midnight on 12 February 1835, Vigny was able to note in his journal: *'Chatterton* a réussi'. The play was a triumph. It had thirty-five performances at the Comédie Française before transferring to the Odéon, and was revived four times during Vigny's lifetime. It has established its place in the repertory of the French theatre and notable modern revivals include those at the Comédie Française in 1947, at the Théâtre de l'Œuvre in 1956 and at the Théâtre de l'Athénée in 1962.

In his note 'Sur les représentations du drame...' (pp.107-10), Vigny paid tribute to the actors who had ensured his play's first night success, recognising their contribution to the disclosure of the 'second drame' behind the text. I have tried to show that this 'second drame' is not only the extra dimension that the play gains in actual performance, but the contribution of the reader or the audience to the action in perceiving the true significance of Kitty's words and in interpreting the underlying meaning of the play, its debate on the nature of poetry and the place of poets or artists in the social order.

As for the performance, it owed a great deal to Marie Dorval, whose acting Vigny significantly describes as *poétique* (p.109), showing the extension of the word to more than just the writing of poetry; and especially to her famous *dégringolade* when, at the end of the play, she collapsed and tumbled down the steps leading to Chatterton's garret. This theatrical piece of business had been kept secret by Dorval, whom Vigny had expected to stagger down the steps before falling on the last of them. It caused an outburst of enthusiasm in the audience which had already stopped the play briefly with its applause at the end of Chatterton's second monologue (p.100). Marie Dorval was not an outstanding actress but she threw herself (literally) into the part of Kitty and did much to ensure the success of the play.

Despite its triumph, *Chatterton* did not have the immediate

effect of spawning a school of *drames de la pensée*. It did lead to
the creation of a prize for a poor poet by De Maillé, but this was
hardly the major reform in patronage for the arts that Vigny had
advocated: that had to wait for the modern state with its arts
councils and, in some cases, its attempts to use writers as its
clients, foreseen by early critics of Saint-Simon's plans to incor-
porate writers and artists into the state machine. What attracted
most attention at first was not Vigny's advocacy of greater
patronage for poetry, but his apparent defence of suicide by
shifting responsibility for it from the individual to an unjust
society. In its widest connotations, this accusation of society is
probably the most modern aspect of the play. Suicide was still
treated as a crime and criticism of the play's immorality in this
respect, based on religious objections, was backed up by the fact
that 'le bruit des pistolets solitaires' (p.32) was heard once or
twice as young poets, foiled in their literary ambitions, decided
to follow Chatterton's example. But the growing acceptance of
the part played by social conditions in individual acts of
violence, including those against oneself, has taken some of the
ground from under this criticism of Vigny's work and is one
reason why some later writers saw it as 'socialist' in its general
intent. The word is, however, wrongly applied: Vigny may have
recognised some of the ills of industrial society and attacked
them, but he did so from the standpoint of an élitist and an
aristocrat, not of a proto-socialist.

In literature, the real vindication of Vigny's support for a
theatre that appealed to the mind was to come towards the end
of the century in the work of such writers as Ibsen, Shaw and, in
France, Henry Becque and others. It is not easy to detect any
direct influence of Vigny on late nineteenth-century realism and
naturalism in France: the climate of *Chatterton* is distinctively
that of Romanticism. But the play has retained its power to
move audiences and readers, its admirers including Albert
Camus who cited the play in his speech in Stockholm on
receiving the Nobel Prize. The occasion was perhaps apt, since
Nobel's foundation is independent of governments; but his prize
is hardly awarded to writers at the start of their careers and, even
if it had existed in 1770, would have done nothing for

Chatterton. The fundamental problem of identifying genius at the moment when it is really in need of help, is as acute as it was in 1835.

The most profound influence of *Chatterton* is the intangible one of fixing more precisely than anyone had managed to do before a certain image of the poet and a certain idea of poetry. The feeling that the poet was a person cursed rather than blessed by an acute sensitivity had found expression in one form in Byron (or rather in the Byronic image), but was fully realised in *Chatterton* before being further defined by Verlaine in his study of the *poètes maudits.* Baudelaire experienced throughout his life the conviction that he was in some way damned and, though there were personal reasons for this in Baudelaire's case which could be attributed to causes other than his poetic genius, his feeling of damnation haunts some of the most personal and most moving of nineteenth-century poetry. Baudelaire, Verlaine and Rimbaud contributed, in their lives, to confirming an idea of the poet that Vigny had sensed in the partly mythical story of an eighteen-year-old English suicide and realised in his play which he wove around 'un nom d'homme' as much as the man himself.

In identifying poetic genius with a particular type of sensibility, Vigny had also posited the equation of poetry itself with this 'poetic' sensibility. Though a passage in his journal in 1843 asserts that poetry in verse is the only real form of poetry, it goes on to define it as 'un elixir des idées', to claim that 'le vrai poète' alone has the ability to discern these ideas and that 'la science est absolument interdit à la Poésie' (5, p.72). This drastic limitation of the field for poetry, which poets in previous centuries would not have accepted, itself derived from a definition of 'the poetic' which allowed it, despite Vigny's assertion, to be applied to a much wider field than that of mere verse. In the play, Chatterton is presented much more as the vehicle for a 'poetic' view of the world than as an author of poetry. He is a dreamer, a martyr who sympathises with the sufferings of mankind, but not a worker, even in words. From here it is only a step to the assertion that whatever a 'poet' does is 'poetic', and that the poetic sensibility may be divorced altogether from the actual production of poetic works.

It was this that led the twentieth-century poet Jean Cocteau to classify all his work, for its collected edition, as 'poetry', his plays becoming *poésie de théâtre*, his novels *poésie de roman*, etc. One of the latter, published in 1929, is *Les Enfants terribles*, a deliberate attempt to create a modern myth comparable with the tales of Classical mythology and a myth that is essentially that of the Romantic idea of poetry. Paul and Elisabeth, the 'children' of the title, are a brother and sister who create poetry in their lives: their room is the temple of a religion which is that of the poetic spirit; its atmosphere transforms those who have the sensitivity to appreciate it and who come within its orbit. Their religion has its ritual, *le jeu*, which is an abandonment of the conscious mind to a form of poetic inspiration; and its cult objects, *le trésor*, a drawer full of commonplace bits and pieces that they have collected which are transformed, like the words of poetry through metaphor, by being divorced from their everyday, functional significance and hidden in this sacred place.

Because the love between Paul and Elisabeth is incestuous, it cannot be disclosed even to the 'children' themselves, so, like the love between Kitty and Chatterton, it is revealed to the reader but not, until the final scene, to the protagonists. Adolescents at the start of the book, they remain children throughout, because their vision is essentially child-like: they are both very wise and very young, with the purity and innocence of Kitty and the 'marvellous boy'. It is Paul, above all, who controls the poetic atmosphere of the room, but not consciously: lazy, weak (both physically and morally), he needs to do nothing in order to be himself.

The novel is a tragedy and one that hinges (despite the Shakespearean intervention of Elisabeth as Lady Macbeth), like *Chatterton*, on a letter (actually, Cocteau makes it a more modern *pneumatique*) and an opiate. The tragic outcome is prepared both by the appearance of this drug and by such indications as the phrase 'Le suicide est un péché mortel' (*13*, p.52) which the children's friend Gérard discovers scrawled on a mirror. It comes, in fact, when Elisabeth discovers that Paul has

fallen in love with Agathe: her jealously, her condemnation of
Agathe as a bourgeoise who is 'not good enough' for Paul, and
Paul's inability to express his love, are all distant echoes of
Chatterton transformed in Cocteau's imagination and in the
context of his story.

However, it is the final scene which most nearly recalls
Vigny's play. Paul, discovering that Elisabeth has tricked him
and deprived him of Agathe's love, takes the opiate in the room
which the children have reconstructed in a new house by means
of screens, highly suggestive of a stage set. As he lies dying on
the bed, in a pose reminiscent of Henry Wallis's painting of the
dead Chatterton, Elisabeth shoots herself and, as she falls,
carries one of the screens with her in a *dégringolade* like that of
Marie Dorval, 'faisant de la chambre secrète un théâtre ouvert
aux spectateurs' (*13*, p.176). It is in this final moment that the
children's love can be made explicit to them, and only then,
when they are both on the brink of death.

Chatterton is by no means the only literary influence on a
novel which, like Vigny's play, welds its sources into a single
work of art quite independent of them. But the influence of
Chatterton is there, less in the details which I have mentioned
than in the concept of poetry. The children of Cocteau's novel
are not, for the most part, unhappy, nor do they suffer the
poverty and indignity of Vigny's hero: fate miraculously cares
for them and provides the conditions in which their natures can
flourish. But they flourish in silence, communicating their
genius only to those who come within their immediate orbit,
'poetic' in their lives, without ever being 'poets' in any strict
sense of the term. By giving such vivid expression to the concept
of the poetic nature, *Chatterton* had prepared for it to be lifted
away from the field of literature and given an independent
existence.

In Cocteau's novel, as in Vigny's play, this 'Romantic'
conception of poetic genius is contained in a work of 'Classical'
simplicity. The labels 'Classical' and 'Romantic' are a
convenient shorthand to describe some general tendencies in
literature and art; they survive because they are useful, not
because they are in any sense exact. Those who attempt to make

them so usually create more problems than they solve. In the case of *Chatterton*, they have questioned whether the play can in fact be described as a 'Romantic' drama at all, in view of its restraint, its near respect of the unities, its simplicity of structure and similarities between Kitty and the heroines of Classical tragedy. It is certainly important to emphasise these features of the play which do much to establish it as a satisfying work of art and have helped to ensure its survival. But, beyond this, any debate on the precise classification of *Chatterton*, any attempt to situate it on a scale from 'Classical' to 'Romantic', is bound to be sterile. The form of the work may owe something to Vigny's knowledge of French drama of the seventeenth century, but it is dictated too by his need to convey a message and to do so in a way that will oblige the spectator or reader to concentrate on the ideas rather than the action. The spirit of *Chatterton* is unmistakably of its time, a time which, despite the revolutionary nature of its literary ideas, did not propose a clean break with the past. On the contrary, what is typically 'Romantic' about Vigny's play is that it incorporates references to the tragedies of Racine and those of Shakespeare, as well as to the 'bourgeois' drama of the eighteenth century and to melodrama. Its hero sees himself as a Stoic facing his destiny like a Roman; but he is also a monk who writes in the language of the Middle Ages, a period undergoing a revaluation in Vigny's day and, by implication, not despised in *Chatterton* as a desert of mere barbarism (which is how it was still considered by many of Vigny's contemporaries). If Chatterton's genius finds its outlet in a revival of medieval literature, then the Middle Ages must have produced work capable of inspiring genuine poetry. This cultural eclecticism, willing to accept as valid all manifestations of human culture, in any form and from any period, is the only proper context in which to view the so-called 'Classical' elements in the play.

More serious is the problem of reconciling what Vigny would have called 'mind' and 'heart', ideas and feelings. A work for the theatre which is going to realise Vigny's ambition of speaking directly to its audience and involving them in the debate on stage, must convince them of the 'reality' of the characters portrayed. The characters in *Chatterton* have been criticised on the grounds that they are one-dimensional, that we perceive them as spokesmen for certain points of view, not as living human beings. This criticism is partly justified. The Quaker's definition of the characters as *martyrs et bourreaux* is too neat and too simple to apply: he, himself, is too wise and virtuous to be credible, Chatterton is too obviously the Poet, Kitty the pure and virtuous heroine, John Bell the tyrannical husband, Beckford the self-satisfied bourgeois. Lord Talbot, admittedly, does reveal an unsuspected side to his nature on his second appearance and crosses the divide to come to Chatterton's defence, but only Kitty can be said to develop in any way during the course of the play, as we see her love for Chatterton overcoming her upbringing as a submissive and virtuous wife. Even in her case, this development is fairly slight and could be anticipated from the start. The other characters announce themselves on their first appearance and remain essentially unchanged by their experiences.

This lack of depth in the characters is perhaps a necessary consequence of Vigny's attempt to write an intellectual drama, and it leaves us with the strong impression that the figures move about the stage enclosed in their own private cages — a feeling reinforced by scenes of misunderstanding and non-communication such as that where Kitty and Chatterton speak through the intermediary of the Quaker. Having taken up their positions, the characters never really interact or respond very much to each other: at most, they reveal what is already there. The very nature of the love between Kitty and Chatterton precludes its future development and by their deaths they evade the choice that it would have imposed on them. If they had ever had to make that choice, they would perhaps have uncovered something in their natures other than these ideals of the martyred poet and the pure heroine which are all that we see of them. As it is, it is impossible to guess how they would have resolved their dilemma or what they would have become in doing so. Taking the immature solution of suicide (or the ideal one of a broken heart), they never have to face the complications of maturity.

Despite this, there are two reasons why the play remains an outstanding work of drama. The first is the language, which Vigny makes appropriate to his characters and which he uses to create an inner world of meanings and correspondences so that a refined and fairly restricted vocabulary becomes an instrument of considerable power. The second is that the play is recognisably a myth in which we can accept that the characters represent ideas outside themselves and pursue their own courses along predestined lines. This feeling of myth is aided not only by the simplicity of the language. Rather than a vast melodrama on the model of *Hernani* or *Ruy Blas*, this is a compressed work, for quartet rather than full orchestra, introducing, interweaving and recalling its insistent themes.

It would be fascinating to see it revived by an imaginative modern director. The concept of poetry that Vigny defends and his understanding of individual psychology may no longer correspond to those of our own time, but the play has an inner consistency that makes it more than an historical curiosity or a memorial to the Romantic ethos. Its author was perhaps wrong in thinking that he had pioneered a trend in drama when he wrote: 'Cette porte est ouverte à présent...' (p.109); but in another sense his confidence was justified, as the artist is always justified in the realisation that he has created a work of art that will endure even when those who enjoy it have ceased to share the ideas it puts forward. This guide has attempted to show that beneath its relatively simple surface it conceals an intricate structure and in analysing this and the ideological framework of the play, I have tried also to suggest some of the many possible approaches to it.

Bibliography and Sources

EDITIONS OF THE PLAY

1. *Chatterton. Quitte pour la peur.* Introduction by F. Germain (Paris, Garnier-Flammarion, 1968). This is the text used throughout the guide. All page references, indicated by one number in parentheses after the reference, are to this edition. All other references give the number of the work in this bibliography, in italics, followed by the page number.
2. *Chatterton.* Critical edition published by Liano Petroni (Bologna, Pàtron, 1962). A full critical edition, with an introduction and notes.
3. *Chatterton.* Edited by Martin B. Friedman, with an introduction by Henri Payre (Paris, Didier, 1967).
4. *Chatterton.* Edited by Jean Delume (Paris, Bordas, 1969). Two easily-obtainable school editions with useful notes and other material in French.

OTHER WORKS BY VIGNY REFERRED TO IN THE GUIDE

5. *Journal d'un poète.* Extracts edited by B. Grillet (Paris, Larousse, 1951). A text in the well-known Classiques Larousse series.
6. *Lettres inédites...au marquis et à la marquise de la Grange (1827-1861).* Published by Albert de Luppé (Paris, Conard, 1914).
7. *Stello. Daphné.* Edited by F. Germain (Paris, Garnier, 1970).

OTHER SOURCES

8. Ballanche, P.S. *Essai sur les institutions sociales dans leur rapport avec les idées nouvelles* (Paris, Didot, 1818).
9. Bird, C. Wesley. *Vigny's Chatterton. A Study of its Genesis and Sources* (Los Angeles, Lymanhouse, 1941).
10. Byron, George Gordon, Lord, 'The Giaour', in *Childe Harold's Pilgrimage and Other Romantic Poems.* Edited by John D. Jump (London, J.M. Dent, 1975).
11. Chatterton, Thomas. *Complete Works.* Edited by Donald Taylor and B. Hoover (Oxford, Oxford University Press, 1971).
12. ——. *Selected Works.* Edited by Grevel Lindop (Oxford, Carcanet Press, 1972).
13. Cocteau, Jean. *Les Enfants terribles* (Paris, Le Livre de Poche, 1977).
14. Denina, Charles. *Tableau des révolutions de la littérature ancienne et moderne.* French translation by T. de Livoy (Paris, 1767).

15. Hugo, Victor. *Préface de Cromwell suivie d'extraits d'autres préfaces dramatiques.* Edited by P. Grosclaude (Paris, Larousse, 1949).

16. Kelly, Linda. *The Marvellous Boy. The Life and Myth of Thomas Chatterton* (London, Weidenfeld and Nicolson, 1971).

17. Lamoine, Georges. 'Thomas Chatterton dans l'œuvre de Vigny et dans l'histoire', in *Dix-huitième siècle*, No. III, 1970, pp.317-30.

18. Meyerstein, E.H.W. *A Life of Thomas Chatterton* (London, Ingpen and Grant, 1930).

19. Moreau, P. *Alfred de Vigny. Stello, Daphné, Chatterton* (Paris, Tournier et Constans, 1949).

20. Sakellaridès, Emma. *Alfred de Vigny, auteur dramatique* (Paris, Editions de la Plume, 1903).

21. Schlegel, A.W. *Cours de littérature dramatique* (Paris, Paschoud, 1814).

22. Shelley, P.B. 'A Defence of Poetry', in *Shelley's Letters and Philosophical Criticism* (London, Henry Frowde, 1909).

23. Simond, L. *Voyage d'un Français en Angleterre pendant les années 1810 et 1811* (Paris, Treuttel et Würtz, 1816).

24. Staël, Madame G. de. *De la littérature considérée dans ses rapports avec les institutions sociales.* Critical edition by P. van Tieghem (Geneva, Droz, 1959).

25. Thibert, Marguerite. *Le Rôle social de l'art d'après les Saint-Simoniens* (Paris, Librairie des Sciences Economiques et Sociales, 1927).

26. Vico, J.B. *Principes de la philosophie de l'histoire.* Translated by J. Michelet (Paris, Renouard, 1827).

CRITICAL GUIDES TO FRENCH TEXTS

edited by

Roger Little, Wolfgang van Emden, David Williams

1. **David Bellos.** Balzac: La Cousine Bette
2. **Rosemarie Jones.** Camus: L'Etranger *and* La Chute
3. **W.D. Redfern.** Queneau: Zazie dans le métro
4. **R.C. Knight.** Corneille: Horace
5. **Christopher Todd.** Voltaire: Dictionnaire philosophique
6. **J.P. Little.** Beckett: En attendant Godot *and* Fin de partie
7. **Donald Adamson.** Balzac: Illusions perdues
8. **David Coward.** Duras: Moderato cantabile
9. **Michael Tilby.** Gide: Les Faux-Monnayeurs
10. **Vivienne Mylne.** Diderot: La Religieuse
11. **Elizabeth Fallaize.** Malraux: La Voie royale
12. **H.T. Barnwell.** Molière: Le Malade imaginaire
13. **Graham E. Rodmell.** Marivaux: Le Jeu de l'amour et du hasard *and* Les Fausses Confidences
14. **Keith Wren.** Hugo: Hernani *and* Ruy Blas
15. **Peter S. Noble.** Beroul's Tristan *and the* Folie de Berne
16. **Paula Clifford.** Marie de France: Lais
17. **David Coward.** Marivaux: La Vie de Marianne *and* Le Paysan parvenu
18. **J.H. Broome.** Molière: L'Ecole des femmes *and* Le Misanthrope
19. **B.G. Garnham.** Robbe-Grillet: Les Gommes *and* Le Voyeur
20. **J.P. Short.** Racine: Phèdre
21. **Robert Niklaus.** Beaumarchais: Le Mariage de Figaro
22. **Anthony Cheal Pugh.** Simon: Histoire